The Future Is Freelance

THE FUTURE IS

freelance

— KIRSTY HULSE

DISCOVERING THE
POWER AND POSSIBILITIES
OF FLEXIBLE WORKING

R3THINK PRESS

First published in Great Britain 2018
by Rethink Press (www.rethinkpress.com)

© Copyright Kirsty Hulse

Cover image © Adobe Stock / Kanokpol / Bloomicon

CONTENTS

Contents

CONTENTS

For Connor, my one constant

INTRODUCTION
WHY I'M WRITING THIS BOOK

It's my belief, which my personal experiences have routinely validated, that the best way to do something new and scary in life is simply to close your eyes and jump.

Life has a tedious way of ensuring that there's always time to worry about formalities and details, but for now, let's just start. This belief is something which I hope to impart throughout the rest of this book, so I'll lead by example and get to writing it.

I'll start by introducing myself and giving you some context on why I'm currently sat at my kitchen table, a little bit tipsy, writing a book on quitting my job, going freelance, and scaling a large business using only independent, remote resource.

It's October 2016 and, like so many other people in modern Western society, I hate my job. It isn't a passionate, acute hate, but the systematic dull ache of sitting on a crowded bus for forty minutes every morning to turn up promptly at an artificially lit office, to be *managed effectively*, and to live the greater part of my life with several people I wouldn't even invite to dinner.

Sound familiar? Maybe that's why you're reading this. I hope you're tipsy, too.

It's only in retrospect I feel so strongly. At the time, I was subtly melancholy about the whole affair but accepted it as my unavoidable reality. Like everyone else, I was under societal pressure to have a *career*, I had bills to pay, a lifestyle to fund, and ambition and drive. Working a nine-to-five job and climbing the corporate ladder was what I'd presumed my life would be, without ever really questioning it.

I grew up in a large family in Stoke-on-Trent. I have four older brothers, all of whom have big personalities and talents. As the youngest and the only girl, I sometimes felt a little lost in all the noise. I didn't have a clear idea of what I wanted to do, and tried many things, never really finding the place into which I felt I truly fitted.

But this feeling ended when I started my career.

I was working for a digital marketing agency, in SEO (search engine optimisation), helping some of the world's largest brands become more profitable by appearing higher in search results. Companies would pay the agency often very large sums of money to make their websites technically sound and trusted by search engines. If you're selling red dresses, for example, and a potential customer is searching for a red dress, being visible to that potential customer is incredibly lucrative, especially since there are billions of consumers making billions of searches every day. The day-to-day of the work is about being technically savvy, understanding code and how the internet fundamentally works, and also about being a creative ad type who understands what kinds of things people want to see and share on the internet. Think Don Draper, but if he were a lot less broody and liked to hack on the side.

For a long time, I loved it. I was good at it, I was making friends, and I was progressing quickly. I found learning how the internet works absolutely fascinating, and threw myself into it with enthusiasm and passion. I was managing a department by the age of twenty-five and, justified or not, the industry began recognising me as being what you might call a 'thought leader'. I got invited to travel across the world to speak at conferences. I moved to London, which, growing up in the economic decline of post-industrial Britain, was as far as my ambitions and dreams could reach. I hit all my predetermined life goals by my mid-twenties, not because I'd done particularly well by society's expectations, but because my ambitions were fairly small.

For the most part, the negatives regarding work at that time were intangible. I was treated decently and paid generously (a dangerous situation to be in if you want to achieve genuine happiness, I think), but I was suffering asphyxiating boredom. Having spent close to a decade in digital marketing agencies, I found the work easy, and there wasn't a huge amount of it.

I was coasting, so to speak. There was little to no stress. No sleepless nights worrying about where my next pay cheque would come from, or how I would manage to get everything done in time. I'd experienced all of that extensively early on in my career, but once I learned how to do my job efficiently, I could breeze through the day. Looking back, it was emphatically restrictive, but you can't know how a small a room is until you've had the opportunity to go outdoors.

One day in early October, I received a text from a close friend with whom I'd worked in the past.

He was head of SEO for a global airline, and was looking for a new agency to hire. He asked me if I had any recommendations. I replied:

'Just get a load of freelancers to work together. It'll be cheaper and they'll do a better job.'

I sent the text, stared at it for a while, and then quit my job the next day to start a digital marketing agency made up entirely of freelance resource, without really thinking about it.

My impulsive, subconscious mind was in the driving seat and I was asleep in the back.

Until the moment I started, and probably for some time after, I had no desire to work for myself. It had never even crossed my mind. In lofty 4am conversations with my friends where we'd discuss our futures and goals and dreams, this was never one of mine. I never identified as an entrepreneur in the way that so many people do. But, there I was, incorporating my business and feeling the crippling anxiety that comes from financial insecurity. At that time, I'd also decided to make the reckless financial decision to rent in London on my own, had around sixty pence in my savings account, and about ten thousand times that in credit card debt. (Let's not even start on student debt – that's still sitting threateningly in an account somewhere).

I had absolutely no capital or financial safety net. The only security I had was that I could, probably, just get another job, should I really, really need to. I would laugh, hysterically, about the risks I was taking as I told my friends and family, thinking that if I just laughed, I could remove the concern and surprise that was etched all over their faces.

I'd like to say that this was an audacious, careless decision under the circumstances, but I don't believe it was. My decision to start my business came out of absolutely nowhere, and it's the best thing I ever did.

Frankly, it was barely even a decision. What it was was one of life's rare and glorious catalytic moments – these moments are likely to be transforming, if you just allow yourself to take a risk. It was the moment that led me to being here. Sitting at my kitchen table, with a glass of red wine, looking out at the London skyline, starting to write a book about working for yourself.

Two years ago, I was invited to pitch for a large contract against many huge, established agencies. A close friend was running it, and he was intrigued by the freelance-only model. The pitch process was formal: I was given a detailed brief, which told me to prepare a presentation and then present it to several key stakeholders. I decided to go ahead, viewing this as an opportunity to take my new idea for a spin. Given that at this point I had no team, or credibility, I pitched alone – just me and my idea that a team of independent, remote freelancers working together would do a great job.

I felt absolutely ludicrous for even going. I thought it offensive, almost, to waste people's time this way, to present an idea that hadn't been validated to a room full of people who were hearing pitches from some of the most successful digital marketing agencies in the world. I hadn't incorporated a business, I hadn't registered a domain, I didn't have a bank account or an accountant. I had nothing.

My idea and I won the pitch.

I'm not sure how. Perhaps it was just the intrigue of something new, or that I was almost certainly significantly cheaper than the competition. Or maybe, just *maybe*, I did something well, but my imposter syndrome will prevent me from ever thinking that. I know I was nervous, and when I'm nervous I speak quickly and make bad jokes, so perhaps that just came across as enthusiastic animation. Unlikely.

I remember getting the email that I won, and again, laughing hysterically to myself and frantically sending out emails to all of my friends all over the world who had gone freelance. Fortunately, throughout my time working in SEO, I'd built up a network of some of the most talented professionals in the industry, so I managed to pull together a strong team, perhaps the industry's best at the time, with relative ease.

Fortunately, when you become a supplier to a large brand, you're often subjected to a thorough procurement process. And this procurement process actually serves as a wonderful checklist for setting up a business.

'Do you have indemnity insurance?'

'Erm...' *Googles indemnity insurance. Buys indemnity insurance.* 'I DO NOW!'

This process was the ultimate exercise in fake it until you make it. Blagging my way through a rigorous process to check that my company, which was yet to be formed, had a robust security protocol for global data protection was completely absurd. No, our IT team did not have a data-protection arm – our IT team was the Gmail tab I had open in my browser.

But fortune favours the brave, or perhaps more truthfully, the scrappy. Two years on, at the time of writing, I'm proud to say that this company is still a client.

Managing to retain them, and keep them happy, under these circumstances makes me incredibly proud, altogether a little surprised and very amused.

This is not my victory to claim, though. It's the victory of my team, the freelancers I work with. My hunch that freelancers working together would do a brilliant job was correct.

Freelancers, in my now fairly developed experience, are happier in their work. They get to pick their child up from nursery. They get to choose whom they work with and what they do. They get to manage their own time. Their output, the projects they work on, is their business and their reputation. As a result, deadlines don't get missed, creativity flows, and people are happy. This is a wonderful reality for both the freelancer and the business that chooses to employ them. And I believe this reality is going to transform the world of work as we know it in the coming decades.

This is why those who have even an inkling of interest in being their own boss should quit their day job and try it out. It's also why businesses need to quickly and efficiently adapt to working with freelancers and encourage remote and flexible working in their employed teams – this is how they'll retain staff and stay relevant.

Just as I had no idea how to run an agency, I have no idea how to write a book. But, here we are.

This book isn't a manual for freelancers or a practical resource explaining what to do and what to expect. This book is a collection of my experiences. It's about my successes, my mistakes, and my motivations. My ultimate aims are to make you laugh, to help you feel excited about taking risks and less afraid of failure, and to showcase the significant business potential of remote working, managing your own time, and, if necessary, ticking yes to that question about your robust security protocol.

But first, some context...

CHAPTER ONE
THE EVIDENCE

The freelance market is booming, and it will only get bigger.

The digital age has paved the way for independent, remote working. For the first time in human history, we can conduct our work anywhere in the world and collaborate across continents. We need only a laptop, cloud storage, and good Wi-Fi. We don't need a formal office space.

As a result, we are increasingly expecting more freedom from our working environments. It no longer makes sense for office-based work to be conducted exclusively in office environments.

As more and more employees question why they need to be strapped to their desks for forty hours a week to get things done, more and more of us will choose to work for ourselves in a freelance capacity. As a result, employers will need to provide flexible, remote working to hire, and retain, the best staff.

Google Trends allows us to see the popularity of a given search term in a particular time period. In September 2012, the popularity score for people searching 'work remotely' worldwide was 20 (out of 100). In September 2017, it was 100, the most popular it has ever been.

This desire to work remotely will continue to rocket, and if employers deny employees this opportunity, they will only succeed in making them feel less satisfied. Adding benefits or putting more beer in the Friday fridge won't cut it. The desire to work away from the office is spreading through society, and this desire will become more culturally ingrained. It's what quality, talented employees will look for in potential employment. As a business owner, there's nothing you can do aside from developing a process to build remote working into your culture, at least occasionally.

Those of us who are tediously Instagramming our laptops in a forest or on the beach are creating an understanding that professional fulfilment can be achieved remotely and self-sufficiently. And as more people begin to adopt this lifestyle, this understanding will be increasingly built into people's desires, and into the idea of what it means to 'be successful'.

It's now, then, that large corporations need to build a structure for remote working into their processes and hiring policies. Otherwise, they risk losing key staff in the coming years and decades. As a result, I've spent several months building a training programme to help service-based corporations shed the mentality that they need a centralised team to be profitable, efficient, and scaled, and to help small business owners understand that scaling up doesn't necessarily mean traditional hiring (I'll cover this later).

GET REAL

Working for yourself isn't easy, and it certainly isn't for everyone. The grave honesty in this book might even put you off 'the dream'. That said, being your own boss is incredibly rewarding, and will be increasingly commonplace in the years to come. I share my experiences of working for myself, and scaling a business using only freelance resource (despite every bit of advice telling me I needed to hire), to try to address honestly the reality of self-employment, both its opportunities and difficulties. It's important that we continue moving into a world of remote working with a clear understanding of its challenges and what's required to efficiently reap its rewards.

The shift to standardising remote working isn't only a cultural one, but also a logistical one. Those who wish to go freelance, set up for themselves, and work remotely need to understand the implications this will have on their time and wellbeing in the short term, and be equipped with the tools to manage and mitigate the stress that can come with being your own boss. Chapters Three, Four, and Five will hopefully help with this. Likewise, businesses need to be prepared for this shift. They must recognise the reality of the marketplace and create a structure that will allow them to develop remote teams and reap the benefits of a freelance workforce. Chapter Six will cover this.

Whether or not you want to work for yourself, the reality is that, as we continue moving into a completely connected, global society, the future is freelance. We need to be prepared for it.

CHAPTER TWO
On Success

I thought it would make sense to start by talking a little bit about the success, and the less-than-success, I've had to date. In my mind, there are two types of success.

External success

The first is external success, which is what most business-centric content focuses on – that is, how much money you make and, consequently, the lifestyle that you can afford.

In my first two years of business, I had a surprising amount of external success. After I secured the global airline as the first client, the business grew rapidly. About sixteen months in, my team and I had nearly twenty clients, many of whom were huge household brands. We were working with global tech corporations, social media platforms, and ecommerce stores. I grew a powerful network of talented, independent resource to rely on to service our clients, and began to develop a process and system to deliver it. In a nutshell, the business took off and nobody was more surprised than I was. Having few overheads, we could be a lot cheaper than the competition; low cost for high quality wasn't especially hard to sell, and the work we were delivering was, for the most part, best in class (skip to Chapter Six to read about when it really wasn't).

I thought I'd solved the problem of finding and keeping good staff, and delivering good work without huge cost, and would continue to grow the business into a global behemoth and live my life out on some Caribbean island drinking piña coladas while watching the performance of my latest investments on my VR headset. I envisaged gleaming offices, immaculate dress, and expensive champagne with all my equally successful immaculately dressed friends, as though I could become the living manifestation of every 'working woman' cliché I'd hungrily consumed in my teen years. Maybe I would change my name to Carrie.

With success, though, I did begin to change. I started to travel first class, buy designer clothes, and get my roots done more often (frankly, I should have been doing them more often for years). My best friend, as all worthwhile best friends should do, got us both drunk and told me I was changing and that he wasn't sure if he liked it. I'd become successful, off my own back, quickly and, as it would transpire, deceptively easily. I felt, in certain moments, incredibly powerful. The people around me were astounded by what I was managing to achieve, single-handedly, at twenty-seven years old with no previous business experience and zero capital. And so was I.

I was rocketing my way to becoming a millionaire.

But I was also unhappy and lonely and isolated.

I'll discuss at length the isolation and psychological exhaustion that comes from being a business owner throughout this book. While I had a lot of external success, it was providing zero growth opportunities for me as an individual. It was taking all of my time and draining me of every ounce of energy.

I was rocketing my way to becoming a millionaire in a midlife crisis.

The more I thought about it, the more I came to realise something. Success, for me, isn't about what I do when I'm working. It's about what I do when I'm *not* working. I was giving all of my spirit and vigour to growing a business, and there was little left for my friends, my family, and myself. Interestingly, I was looking through some old photos the other day and noticed that at that time, right in the throes of new-business mayhem, I'd put on quite a lot of weight. That's not interesting in and of itself. I've spent a lifetime happily managing and mismanaging my cheese addiction. What I found surprising was that *I hadn't noticed*. I had no idea, at the time, that I'd stress-eaten my way to two stone heavier because I wasn't paying any attention to myself.

Some people thrive on the fight of the grind and the potential for swathes of external success. For me, being self-sufficient and financially independent is of course rewarding, but it's not what I really care about, at my core. I've found my 'why', and it turns out it's staying in bed eating crumpets.

Ask anyone who knows me, and they'll say that I tragically undersell myself – that I don't openly talk about my success and that I intentionally dumb down what I've achieved to the point of it being annoying and, frankly, a little bizarre. I won't deny this. This is perhaps the first time I've admitted that I've had external success. When people ask me what I do, I generally shrug and say 'marketing' and deflect the question. If they probe, I say, 'I run my own business. It's okay.'

Amusingly, my husband likes to recount that for months, he had no idea what I did for a career, and only found out when he overheard a conversation between his friend and me. I never told him any details, and merely gave him enough scraps of information to satisfy him. He knew and accepted that I ran my own business, and that it was okay. I've thought deeply about my reasoning for this, and it comes down to a few factors, which I'll discuss later in the book. Primarily, the reason I never talk about work if I can avoid it is because it's never quite felt like *me*, and I certainly don't want to be defined by it.

Internal success

That leads me to the second type of success: internal success – that is, the feeling that you're doing what you like to do, dedicating your time to something that matters, that's important to you and that doesn't just pay the bills but also makes you feel proud of yourself. This kind of success is a real luxury, something which most people accept to be out of reach. And perhaps unsurprisingly, selling digital marketing strategies to massive brands wasn't *exactly* ticking that box for me. I had lots of external success, and I found temporary enjoyment in the exercise of seeing what I could do if I really pushed myself. This wasn't going to provide sustainable satisfaction, though.

In the course of growing the business, what I've come to realise is what I do care about, passionately. What I'm happy to shout about from the rooftops (or these pages) is the power of professional autonomy, both for the individual and the business world as a whole.

My success to date has taught me that it's time we reject the notion that you *have* to work in a nine-to-five office environment to be fully productive. That a manager needs to be able to physically see a person's screen to understand their output. That showing up is the same as getting things done. That to scale your business you need to hire. And that the only way to collaborate is to be housed together in bizarre beanbag-laden work prisons for most of our lives.

It's not that we should reject traditional working entirely, but simply that we should reject it being *the only way*. This idea creates gender gaps in our workforce, congests our roads, centralises society, generates huge and often unnecessary expenses for businesses, makes parenting harder than it already bloody is, and implies that we aren't adult enough to manage our own time.

There must be options to work in different ways. For many, the routine and security of office-based work is hugely beneficial. But if, as I do, you think you can stay in bed and eat crumpets and be effective professionally, or you want to scale a business in a cost-effective way and keep your team as happy as possible, then keep reading.

CHAPTER THREE

MANAGING THE FEAR

Whenever someone tells me that they've decided to go freelance, my first question is almost always 'How's the fear?' And it's almost always met with a knowing, nervous laugh.

Those of you who are already freelance will know exactly what I'm talking about. If you want to go freelance but haven't quite mustered the strength just yet, it's likely that 'the fear' is preventing you. 'The fear' is referenced many times throughout the rest of the book, so henceforth, I'll refer to it as TF.

TF is a type of stress that I started feeling only when I decided to go freelance, and it has stayed with me ever since. It's the fear of not being able to feed yourself, or your family; the fear of losing everything you've ever worked for. Ultimately, it's a deep-seated mistrust in your ability to keep generating the revenue that allows you to live. Not only does TF tell you that you're incapable of doing what you set out to do, but also, that you're an arse for even trying.

For me, TF is more visceral than other stresses. I imagine, and I most certainly hope, that this fear is the closest I'll come in modern society to the primitive fight-or-flight response. It's a powerful adrenal reaction that makes me lie in bed some mornings feeling paralysed by the weight of a responsibility too heavy to bear, and a powerful adrenal reaction that makes me vault from bed some mornings feeling an ability so promising it's impossible to ignore.

Picture the fear as an avalanche: sometimes containable and not immediately a threat, other times a gradual, distant threat, and in the worst of times, a threat so spontaneous and rapid and powerful you feel the need to run. But this desire to run is often what propels me in to action.

I'll give you an example.

Ask any of my closest friends and they'll confirm that my twenties were largely a tearless few years of little emotional turbulence (or at least outward emotional turbulence). Then, the moment I decided to go freelance, I got into the unhelpful habit of weeping like an overtired toddler every Monday morning. Every Monday morning, at about 9.30am, you could set your clock to the sounds of my sobs. My neighbours probably thought something horrific was happening, and they'd have been right – I was learning about taxes.

It went like this. I would get out of bed on Monday, often in a good mood, feeling confident and excited for the week. I would make coffee, sit down, calmly, in front of my laptop, and get to writing my to-do list. And then, seemingly out of nowhere, I would crumble. Crumble like a biscuit left too long in tea. Crumble into a soggy, lifeless mess. I'd usually weep at my computer screen muttering something incoherent: 'I... I... But... I... can't.' Occasionally, I'd try to pep myself up with a shower, though this often just spurred on the tears.

I would remain a soggy, lifeless mess for about an hour before I managed to contain myself, usually by listening to Prince and my then project manager and now close friend Josh.

Josh helped me figure out why Monday mornings were so difficult – I was starting my week with admin. The logic was reasonable: get set up and organised for the week ahead by sorting my finances and to-do lists. As it turns out, finances and to-do lists are what I find most difficult. So, combine what I find hardest with Monday morning (which softens even the hardest of us) and I was nothing more than a drowned digestive in the bottom of a mug.

The excellent news was that this was a relatively easy fix. I simply started doing my admin on Friday afternoons, when the pressures were a little lighter and I could play music and have a gin. Gin and tonic and accounts on a Friday afternoon is celebratory. Gin and tears and accounts on a Monday morning is a cry for help.

I still hate doing admin, and it will always create a swell of anxiety, but now that swell doesn't break into a wave of despondency. The absurd Monday-morning weeping has abated, and my emotional outbursts have since been reigned back into a healthy British reserve. And rightly so.

Although my weekly weeping has stopped, TF is still often triggered when I do something that I've never done before. It feeds on the unknown, both intangible – the future seems a little less defined when you're freelance – and tangible – that moment when you're filing your first tax return or desperately Googling 'indemnity insurance'. Honestly, does anybody actually know what indemnity insurance is? Probably not.

Going freelance or starting your own business is often a series of unknowns, one after the other. The good news is that every time you get through a tax return, or buy your first year's indemnity insurance, you add to personal arsenal of experiences. Thus, things aren't quite so scary anymore. Like everything else in life, these things get easier over time – not in the sense of work required, but in how it feels to get up and start this work.

Two years into being freelance, I'm much better at managing TF, simply because I acknowledge it's there and recognise that often, it can be quite helpful. I don't believe that we can ever really overcome the fear, but I do believe we can learn to manage it and use it to our benefit. To do this though, we need to understand what type of fear is being felt.

In my experience, there are two distinct types of fear: practical and impractical.

Practical fears are often financial or logistical: the fear that you won't have enough money to pay rent, that your idea might not be the great money spinner you'd hoped, that you'll lose your house, or that you won't be able to maintain enough revenue to keep your staff.

Impractical fears, however, are more often twinned with a sense of self: the fear that you'll fail and look stupid, that you don't deserve success (a personal favourite), or that you just aren't good enough.

In my experience, practical fears are a rational response to real-world, objective threats. Impractical fears are an irrational response to self-created, subjective threats.

So how do you overcome them?

OVERCOMING IMPRACTICAL FEARS

I'm lucky enough (or unlucky enough, depending on your position) to be a risk-taker. This means that the common, impractical fears that my friends and family so often suffer from seem to be less of a problem for me. I have many characteristics that require managing to ensure I'm achieving in the way I want to (that is, to ensure I'm finishing what I start, mostly), but I've a natural gung-ho attitude that I imagine can be absolutely infuriating.

Given the option to try something new and precarious or something safe and certain, I will, within the reasonable confines of wanting to remain alive, choose the former. Not through ambition or bravery, but through an arguably naive prioritisation of risk and jeopardy – the things in life that affirm us.

Simply put, I would rather try and fail than not try at all. (I do, of course, grimly await the day that this mindset comes back to bite me in the arse, but so far, so good.) I've always wanted to be the person who dies with a small smile and sense of pride – not because I achieved everything that I ever wanted to achieve (we should all be kinder to ourselves than that), but because I *tried* everything I wanted to *try*.

Merit isn't only in our successes, but also in our attempts.

The fear that prevents us from taking risks in business (and life in general) is often a deep-seated fear of judgement or failure. When I first started Manyminds, the main demon I had to fight was the fear of ruining my 'reputation'. I was petrified that I would start a business that wouldn't work, and that all my peers would automatically think that I wasn't actually very good at my job at all – as a result, I'd never be invited to speak at conferences again, my friends in the industry would disown me, and all the work and effort I'd put into being respected and liked would be wasted. I would never be able to find work again, and would be left on the shelf a *ruined woman*. I'd live out the rest of my life alone and ashamed in a bonnet on a cruel uncle's country estate, the laughing stock of the village. This failure would overwrite every good and positive thing I'd ever done in my career to date, including the gumption to set up a business in the first place, and would forever prevent me from finding employment.

It sounds a little absurd, doesn't it?

Try writing out your deepest fears. Break them out into practical and impractical, and see if the impractical fears seem absurd, too. Once you've established exactly what your impractical fears are, it's easier to overcome them.

To overcome our impractical fears, we have to give weight and power to simply trying. My experience has taught me that 'try', this small, unassuming three-letter word, is perhaps the most powerful, motivating, and soothing word at our disposal.

I know that in many circles this is a statement punishable by death, but Yoda, you're wrong. Yoda, you're wrong when you say, 'Do or do not. There is no try.'

Trying is our first, unintimidating step into the unknown. The small, unassuming word 'try' is the David to the powerful Goliath that is our impractical fears.

I often see people outright refuse to attempt things for fear of not completing them or not being any good at them. To those, I can offer the innocuous strategy of simply trying. If we're asking ourselves only to try, then we're reducing the crushing pressure of needing to complete or succeed. Of course we want to complete or succeed. But at this stage, the most important goal is simply the trying. With an attempt may come completion or success, but there's no pressure, only opportunity.

If we convince ourselves that the value is in simply having a go, then we can better manage our impractical fears, our fears that tell us we're not good enough, or that it will never work. The first step is only to try. And if you do that, you've succeeded.

Many of you might now be thinking, 'But what if I try and then fail?'

Remember, we've already established that merit isn't only in our successes, but also in our attempts.

Think of something you've always wanted to try. It could be anything – life drawing, asking someone on a date, going freelance, baking gluten-free blueberry muffins, whatever. Then consider the thoughts that have prevented you from trying this thing. I firmly believe that if you have even a semblance of an interest in trying something, you'd better give it a go to avoid deathbed regrets, to avoid whispering 'I could have' to a room full of saddened onlookers.

In writing this book, I thought a lot about where my 'let's just try' mentality came from, in order to reverse-engineer some advice for those on the cusp of trying something new.

It didn't take me long to know what the answer was.

I was one of those intolerable stage kids. I spent my childhood on a Stoke-on-Trent stage in sequins, never quite able to do the splits. Despite years of effort in dance classes, I was so bad at it. Like, really bad. Terribly, awfully, not even adorably, bad.

I was inflexible, clumsy, not good at remembering the steps, and, for the most part, cripplingly self-conscious. My mum has an *amazing* VHS of a gym routine where all the other boys and girls glide and bend across the stage – graceful and lithe – before a glorious finale of cartwheeling in a diagonal line to a crowd of adoring parents.

I bring up the back – stiff and stout – and do a single, sad bunny-hop to a crowd of pitying parents (and my mum, who somehow managed to remain both straight-faced and consistently pleased with my output).

When I watch now I cry with hysterical laughter, but there are some real tears in there too, because I'm still, after all, that chubby little girl who was *really* embarrassed and felt very small.

That feeling is one that was fairly symptomatic of my childhood. I by no means had a bad time: my family are loving, I had whatever I wanted (apart from a Mr Freeze that I'm still waiting for as fifth-birthday gift from my brothers), and I was given unconditional support and encouragement to pursue, or quit, any of my whims at any time. By myself, I felt happy and well rounded, but in groups, I became overwhelmingly shy.

I was much fatter than and not as pretty as the other girls. I wasn't in their 'group', probably because I offered little other than looking at my feet during breaks and theirs during lessons. I struggled to make friends, wet the bed for probably longer than I should have, and queued for the tuck shop even when I didn't have any money because I didn't want people to see I was alone.

Within that lonely, awkward girl, though, was a show-off desperately seeking attention. At about this time I played a game called Dead. It was a largely solitary game where I'd lie motionless on the floor for as long as it took for someone to panic and come to my aid. Or, more often, for my mum to say, 'Kirsty, get up. We know you're not dead.' I was a girl who didn't want to go unnoticed. I wanted to be seen and heard; I just hadn't quite worked out how to do that yet.

I don't think I'm unique in this way. All children, and probably adults, too, are just ill-formed weirdos who haven't worked out what on earth is going on yet and think that playing dead is an appropriate way to define themselves as thoughtful, conscious beings. For those of you still experimenting, get up. It isn't.

My desire to be heard led me to performing, and this performing had different guises over the years. I danced, badly. I acted, terribly. I played the cello, appallingly. All the while being fantastically shy. My parents were probably frustrated, probably hoping I'd find something I actually liked one day, but they went along with it all, regardless. My dad ferried me across Staffordshire to county choir on Mondays, and to more recorder festivals than any metal fan from the Midlands should have to bear. But in the fleeting moments I decided that a career in a Baroque chamber orchestra, or in a West End chorus, or in a gospel choir was my one true destiny, my parents thought, 'So be it.'

The start bit, where I'd have to walk in and talk to the other people in the group – horrendous. But when the lights and music came on, I became my own, sorry, Sasha Fierce.

Macclesfield drama festival, 1996. I don't think I've ever felt more fear in my entire life. I was sitting in a school hall with some crumpled notes in my lap eating a Twix with shaking hands. I had to deliver a monologue on stage any minute. There were trophies to be won, and I'd been memorising it for weeks. It was an excerpt from *The BFG*. I liked that book. I could memorise the words, but I wasn't good at acting them out. I spoke too quickly and my voice got shaky. I just needed to get it over with. Then it would be done, and I would feel good, and my mum would get me a *Boyzone* magazine and a Flump. Even if I messed it up, it would be fine because it was the taking part that counted.

'It's the taking part that counts, isn't it, Mum?'

'Yes, duck, just do your best.'

My best! I could do my best! And I did. I went on the stage, in front of a big crowd and judging panel, and I did my best.

My best was shit.

I can't really remember how it went, though I do distinctly remember not winning but still feeling triumphant. Probably because it was over, and my mum was proud, and I had a Flump.

I always knew, very clearly, that I wasn't as good as the other children I was learning and performing with (apart from when I played Nancy [in *Oliver!*] – I was *born* to play Nancy). I remember once when I was about seven or eight going to the toilet during ballet class. While trying to negotiate a too-tight leotard and tights, I overheard the girls in the next cubicle giggling about how bad I was. I crisply remember a sense of naive indignation.

I knew I was bad, but why were they being so mean? I was having fun! What did it matter to them if I couldn't remember the steps? Give me another five years and that naive indignation would become a clear 'fuck you'.

I hid in the toilet, waited for them to leave, and went back to class resolved to show them that I didn't care what they thought. They weren't going to ruin my fun. I was having a go and being heard, which is really all I cared about.

I guess that was a benefit of growing up in a large family of boys; I quickly learned to brush off the taunts and focus on just having fun. My brothers weren't especially mean – they were just older brothers. They used to play a 'game' called Fifty-Two-Card Pickup. I'd get so excited for the rare opportunity to be included in their card game. What actually transpired was they threw all the cards on the floor and made me pick them up. They found it hilarious. I found it emotionally crushing. I quickly learned to stop giving a shit if other people were laughing at me.

Ultimately, in those tender, formative years, I accidentally stumbled upon the skill of not basing my self-worth on comparisons to others. I perpetually thrust myself into terrifying situations because I knew that there was value in just *trying* – I knew that if it went wrong, it really didn't matter, and it never turned out to be quite as scary as it first seemed. For me, that took the form of awkward dancing and tuneless piano playing. But it could be needlework, sports (never tried them), or anything that requires you do your best, and nothing more.

Our best is all we ever have, and sometimes, our best won't cut it. But once we've tried, we've already succeeded in giving ourselves a chance be heard. We've stood in our own little spotlight. In our professional lives, as much as in school, it really is the taking part that counts.

All that matters is that we sign up and take part.

Impractical fears come from the deepest places in our hearts. They're often woven into who we are as people. They come from our upbringings, our experiences, and our environments. For many, including me, the fear of failure is a real, and unavoidable, part of life. But you need not let this fear control who you are today.

Another impractical fear that I have to manage is the fear of success. A fear of success might sound strange, but I don't think it's uncommon. We all have an idea of ourselves, a category we put ourselves in, so that we can navigate the world around us. From an evolutionary standpoint, stereotyping is a helpful way to make swift decisions about whether we're in danger. For me, becoming a successful business owner wasn't within my category. Failing was within my category. I'd adjusted to that and become a confident and robust failure from a young age. I'd never viewed myself as capable of being a business owner – I never thought I was brave enough, or driven enough, or serious enough. I joke my way through life and couldn't reconcile that with my perception of the serious entrepreneur. Before starting Manyminds, the idea of success made me question my identity. Would I still be the same me? I wasn't sure what an austere, prosperous Kirsty looked like. Maybe I'd wear a monocle. Maybe I'd start taking myself seriously. I couldn't picture myself in that position, and it confused and scared me.

I went to see a business coach in the summer of 2017. At this point the business was going better than I'd ever expected – I had happy clients, and for the first time in my life, I was wealthy. I didn't have a monocle, though I did buy some designer sunglasses in the airport before a business meeting in Dublin and felt like Jay-Z. I hadn't considered seeing a coach before, but he was a close friend of my husband, so I thought I'd try it. The accuracy of his question at the end of the session surprised me.

'Are you from a working-class background?'

'I guess,' I replied.

I'd not mentioned anything about my background in the session – I'd merely spoken about how my business had grown and I wasn't sure where to take it next. He pointed out that my main problem was that I was still stuck in the execution of the business. I wasn't taking any risks to step beyond that; I wasn't investing anything or making broader strategic decisions about the future of the business. I had remained, as it were, a worker.

I was, and in many ways still am, reluctant to take the step into ownership. Making overarching decisions about investment and growth, rather than doing the hard grind of the day-to-day, feels out of my category. I've never learned about investments or IPOs or business strategy. It's all a foreign currency to me. Getting clients, and doing some work, and keeping clients happy – that's where I'm comfortable. And as my business grows and the risks change, I still fear success, and feel uncertainty about stepping outside of what I've always thought to be my station. This is something I'm aware of and working on (hence why I'm writing this bloody book, I guess). It's undeniable that sometimes, we'll struggle to push ourselves because we're afraid of losing our core identity and can't envisage how we'll be when we step outside of the category we've defined for ourselves.

In this instance, asking yourself to try doesn't really help. When it's not failure but success that we're afraid of, and this fear is ultimately holding us back, we need a different strategy. My personal fear of success comes largely from a sense of feeling undeserving. I feel I don't deserve happiness, and if I do get it, I feel the need to constantly ensure I'm earning it. But how I overcome my fear of success is simple – I make time to consciously and actively enjoy the successes I've had to date. I travel, or go shopping, or take an afternoon nap. Taking time to enjoy what you've achieved so far, whether this means buying a new plant for the home you love, or taking yourself to the cinema one evening, helps you to stop being so afraid of what could be ahead.

IMPOSTER SYNDROME

Alongside my fear of future success is a fear of my current success, which I recognise as imposter syndrome. I get imposter syndrome *a lot*.

By imposter syndrome, I mean that weird sense of objectively seeing yourself achieving and doing good things but, internally, not really understanding *how* you're doing them. This is underpinned by a consistent, subtle ebb of fear that it will inevitably all come crashing down at any moment. It's like an out-of-body experience in which you're acting as a person you don't really feel like. Sometimes it's faint, barely there at all; and other times, typically when we've won a new client or are doing really great stuff, it kicks in full force.

Here's a good example. About a year into the business, my freelance team and I had a spate of client wins. We'd been successfully operational for some time at this point, so had developed a few strong case studies, but were still new enough to be intriguing (and cheap), and got invited to pitch for a string of big-name brands. To my utter amazement, we won them all. I remember one telephone call in particular – I was told we'd won the contract, and my heart sank. I distinctly remember the feeling. It was one of loss and fear. A feeling of unease in the pit of my stomach similar to the one I feel when a relationship is turning sour, or when I'm nine years old and have been caught stealing ten pounds from my mum to buy Spice Girls stickers (I still harbour extreme guilt about this). The feeling was imposter syndrome. I couldn't feel proud of or delighted by the success my business – *my* business, *my* idea, grown by *me* – was having because it all just felt too absurd. This couldn't possibly last. I'd get found out as the disorganised, hapless mess I am soon enough and it would all come cascading down around me.

My imposter syndrome is like a mini, heavy-breathing Darth Vader on my shoulder whispering to me that I'm going to mess things up. Thankfully, I've also got a mini, charming Captain Kirk on my left shoulder reassuring me that all objective experience and evidence suggests otherwise, and I can command the *Enterprise*! Or something.

My struggle is that it seems like only five minutes ago I was spending my Saturday afternoons hanging out in a Tesco car park in Stoke-on-Trent wearing ripped baggy jeans and a Slipknot hoodie, failing *majestically* at learning the tabular chords to 'Smoke on the Water'. I still feel, internally, like that awkward teenager who had barely worked out how to run a bath, let alone a business.

But imposter syndrome, much like other fears, can be helpful. My fear of everything crashing down ultimately prevents this from happening.

For example, walking into a room and acutely *not* feeling like the smartest person makes me open to opinions and advice. I know for a fact I would never have got Manyminds to where it is today without desperately sniffing out opinions like a somewhat-less-than-graceful pig sniffing for truffles. Being acutely aware that those around me are experts, and intelligent, makes me a better listener, makes me more open to feedback, and makes me better at seeing the reality of a situation from multiple perspectives.

Constantly feeling the need to check in and make sure I'm not about to mess everything up makes me constantly check in and make sure I'm not about to mess everything up. The subtle worry that people might think I'm not good enough means I work really hard to try to prove my (and Manyminds') value. Having moments of uncertainty about what I'm *actually* good at allows me to contribute in ways that are *actually* helpful, and to delegate to those who are good where I am most definitely not.

Knowing that I work in an industry brimming with capable, intelligent, competent people means I push relentlessly to ensure my business doesn't fall below the standard.

The best thing about imposter syndrome, though, is that when I feel it most profoundly, I turn to my friends, or my team, and tell them I really don't know what I'm doing – and then everybody admits that they don't either.

In business, fear is one of the most practical tools. Once we take our first step (trying), the day-to-day fears involving not being able to manage what we've chosen to take on are what propel us into action.

The very reason I'm here now, writing this book, is down to a fear of falling behind the curve, of being one of the first people to start a freelance-only marketing agency but not putting my stake in the ground to claim it. I'm here writing this book because I had a fear of getting usurped.

If we can just ask ourselves to take small steps to enjoy current and hypothetical success, then our impractical fears stand less of a chance of bringing us down, and our practical fears can carry us through to the finish line.

Overcoming practical fears

Practical fears are much more, well, practical. They are often what drive us, motivate us, and give us that extra push we need to avoid procrastination or laziness. I've developed a healthy respect for practical fears over the years. Without them, I wouldn't have won that new client. I wouldn't have spoken at that conference. I wouldn't have started a business.

Without those moments of feeling practical, manageable fears, I wouldn't have done most of the things that have brought me success in my business to date.

Practical fears are more easily managed than impractical fears as they aren't about sense of self but objective facts. Thus, they can be objectively managed. Let's break down the practical fears most freelancers face.

I DON'T KNOW HOW TO SET UP A BUSINESS!

This is one of the most common fears. It's a practical fear in the sense that it's accurate – when you do something for the first time, you don't know how to do it. But if you're telling yourself this, it's probably just an excuse, and there are much bigger, more impractical fears preventing you from starting. The level of admin required might seem intimidating, but it's surprisingly easy. A lot of people get bogged down in choosing a name when they first start, but this is unhelpful and distracting. The right name will come to you over time. Don't obsess over it as your first thing. I originally incorporated my business as Kirsty Hulse Ltd (narcissist, I know) then used the trade name Manyminds for the first year or so, until I knew it was right and got round to formally changing it – let me rephrase: got round to emailing my accountant to ask him to formally change it. You don't even have to set up a limited company or form a business if that feels intimidating. You can simply decide to be a sole trader and let HMRC know.[1] Honestly, it really is that easy.

Don't let the admin get in the way of your starting. Government websites provide lots of easy-to-follow guidance.

Of course, if you're like me and even the thought of admin is debilitating (seriously, I didn't change my name after marriage for this very reason) and truly preventing you from taking the first step, I recommend you get your phone out of your pocket, Google 'accountants near me', click on a name you like the sound of, and email that person, right now, saying nothing more than 'I'm thinking of starting a business. Can you help?' Then the admin is out of your hands. If you can do this one small act, you'll set the ball rolling, and there you have it – you're freelance. Congratulations!

WHAT IF THERE'S ANOTHER RECESSION?

I've heard this one a few times as well, and I understand it completely. Many businesses struggled

---

[1] www.gov.uk/working-for-yourself

to make it through the last big recession, and I acknowledge we all might feel a little safer being employed during turbulent economic times. Still, this shouldn't be a fear preventing you from going freelance, as the risk of having no work is still there whether you're employed or not. Companies can cut back and make redundancies – there is always risk. Freelancers tend to benefit when companies are watching costs more scrupulously, and larger, more costly options can suffer. Ultimately, don't prevent your potential success with a lofty 'what if'.

HOW WILL I GET BUSINESS?

'How on earth will I get business?' is perhaps the first thing you'll ask yourself when deciding to go freelance. Then, once you win your first client, you'll hop on the non-stop business carousel of 'How on earth will I retain my business and get more business?'

There's no guaranteed way of getting business, and I implore you to mistrust anyone who says otherwise. How you successfully generate business will depend hugely on your target market, your product or service, and your price point.

I cannot give you ten magic steps to getting business or three rules to double your revenue overnight, but what I can do is tell you exactly how it works for me, and hopefully some of it will apply to you and your business.

All of my new business is a result of these three things.

1. Networking

2. Doing good work

3. Being genuine

Networking

Manyminds' website is shocking, despite the fact that we're a digital marketing agency. And we've never marketed ourselves (the cobbler always has bad shoes, as they say). I'm increasingly embarrassed when people point out to me that our website doesn't work well on mobile – that's the equivalent of someone pointing out to an accountancy firm they haven't paid their VAT. In all the chaos of starting the business, getting set up in this sense was low on the list of priorities. This was a good problem to have, as we weren't relying on a compelling website or an engaging and insightful Twitter account to generate revenue.

I've never paid for any form of advertising, I don't employ salespeople, and I've never made cold calls or sent sales emails. I might need to employ these tactics one day, and I'm not saying they don't work. I've simply chosen to grow my business in other ways.

We got our first few clients because of the peers I had in the industry – people I'd met over the years. Speaking at conferences was an excellent way for me to meet a lot of people and become relatively well respected. (It's perhaps a bit of a misnomer when I say that I've never marketed my business, because while I've never marketed my business, I have spent years working hard at marketing *myself*. Here I am, at it again.)

When I set up my business, a couple of clients trickled in as a result of the reputation I'd built for myself. I invested a lot of time and effort early in my career networking, writing blog posts on what was happening in my industry, and meeting influential people and speaking at events. This has created huge opportunities for me to grow my business.

However, this may not be practical advice for many of you. It took ten years of standing awkwardly at networking events and terrorising myself by forcing myself to get up on stage and talk about the work I was doing to build a good reputation and wide network (the terror abated to a manageable mild discomfort over time – it always does). At the first event I ever spoke at, there were about seven people in a room above a pub, and I spent weeks in advance feeling sick to my stomach at the thought of it. The night before the event, I lay in bed silently sobbing, envisaging my inevitable failure. I was young and inexperienced, and the thought of speaking in front of people I viewed as infinitely better and more intelligent was legitimately terrifying. But my stage-school ego pulled me towards the crowd, and I'm grateful to my former self for being such a goddamn sadist.

When I moved to London a few years later, I became a tiny fish in a large pond and consequently struggled to be invited to speak at events. Nobody in my industry knew who I was, and I had no idea who they were either, so just as I was starting to build momentum and confidence as a speaker, I found myself without the opportunity to keep practising and growing. I started going to lots of events to try to meet people; I'd buy drinks and email event organisers afterwards in an attempt to build my network, to little avail. After about a year, I was still struggling to be invited to speak anywhere. I became impatient, and I was close to giving up when I had an idea. I solved the problem of not being invited to speak at events by simply organising an event myself and speaking at it. I've always struggled with being told no. It seemed to do the trick, and after that, I kept getting invited to events. I now run a country-wide event whose purpose is to give people the opportunity to speak if they never have. (If you're interested, email me.)

If you have the opportunity, time, and inclination, consider speaking at conferences, events, or meetups. Many conferences offer new speakers the chance to pitch for a slot, and you'll likely find many smaller meetups and events that you can get involved in.

It's worth adding that in general, when it comes to public speaking, you either want to do it or you really don't, and that's fine. I have many friends who have zero inclination to speak at conferences, and they're plagued by guilt and pressure to do so. If you want to, but it's TF that's preventing you, close your eyes and jump in. But if it just doesn't feel right for you, that's OK. Like freelancing, public speaking is a glove that fits some and not others. Alternatives include writing influential and well-thought-out blog content, or being an active and supportive conference attendee, or even just being the last person at the bar – that seems to work wonders too.

Networking outside of your direct industry can reveal a gold mine of new business as well. Try reaching out to previous employers or clients. Anybody who has enjoyed working with you in the past is likely to want to do it again. Speak to family and friends – not necessarily for their business directly (charging for your time gets a little more nuanced when there's shared blood or love involved), but so that they can refer you to anybody they may know. Cast your net wide. The more people you can infect with your enthusiasm (or blatant horror), the more likely it is you'll get a lead.

Doing good work

It may sound trite, but doing good work is one of the most important factors in my business's remaining solvent. First, good work ensures referral business, which allows us to grow. And second, it ensures we can sell our services in a way that's more compelling and believable.

It's not always possible to do good work. Believe me, there's a whole chapter dedicated to my failures later in this book. But thankfully, there's a lot I have to be proud of, so if I focus on the areas my team and I excel in, those things about which I can say, hand on heart, we're better at than the competition, I become a compelling saleswoman. I'm not *selling* anybody anything – I'm just informing them. Tom, who has the unfortunate task of being my right-hand man, calls this the 'stealth sale'. Sometimes I find myself flogging our services without realising it. I simply believe in what we do. You have to.

I always pity the poor marketing manager of a business that just isn't good. I used to work at a tech start-up, and it was one of the most challenging jobs I've ever had. I found it virtually impossible to sell the things I didn't believe in or wouldn't use myself. I would work alongside the marketing team, helping them come up with campaigns that would showcase how magnificent the new product update was, when really it was just a badly stitched button on a dusty old jacket. It doesn't matter what industry you work in – whether you're trying to market scented toilet rolls or luxury holidays, you have to believe that what you're offering is all right, at the very least.

Does this sound familiar? To confidently, and genuinely, sell your services, your first port of call is to believe they're good (and offer competitive and fair pricing). If you're struggling to generate business and can't sincerely say that the work you do is both good and well priced, I suggest addressing this before anything else.

In the early days, my business grew organically through word of mouth and referrals. My team and I were doing genuinely good work for our clients, and, being a freelance-only model, we were a little different from what they were used to, so we continued to get work. If one of our clients left their role, they'd employ us in their new position, or recommend us to their friends and peers. When someone who trusts you refers you to someone else, there's a good chance this referral will result in paid work.

Being genuine

I'm fairly confident that the way I've sold clients on my business is by not trying to actively sell it.

Our first client signed us on a three-month proof of concept. That is, we had three months to prove we could deliver what we were promising. It transpired that we absolutely could not.

Our ducks weren't in a row, we'd bitten off more than we could chew, and we'd made several mistakes simply because we were brand-spanking new. We tried *so hard,* but we blundered around like children playing shop.

In the final few days of that three-month contract, I went in to see our client, fully prepared to accept and acknowledge our failures and likely lose their business. I was incredibly nervous walking into that meeting. I felt embarrassed and insignificant. I felt like a fraud.

In my enthusiasm, I'd promised something we couldn't quite pull off. The bare bones were there, but we lacked the processes and scaled efficiency that come from an established business. And we certainly couldn't provide the kind of slick delivery that a business of this size was used to.

In the meeting, I did what I do in any other situation when I've disappointed someone: I listed all my mistakes and apologised for them (my husband might not agree that this level of humility is an *established* trait of mine, but on that day, it was). I explicitly stated everything we'd done wrong because I couldn't bring myself to try to hide it or make excuses for it. I'd woken up that morning determined to boldly justify *why* we'd made mistakes, though when it came down to it, I didn't have the gumption. I'd been in the agency world too long and just couldn't be bothered. For the past decade I'd worked in agencies where it was standard practice to gloss over mistakes, or tweak numbers to make them look better, or blame mistakes on a third party. I'd started my own business to get away from that. I said that what we'd done was wrong, and I explained how I would fix things, if we were given the opportunity to do so.

At that point, the entire dynamic of our relationship with that client changed. Rather than telling us to get on our bikes, they renewed the contract there and then. I left feeling a little flabbergasted, and I'm forever grateful to Amy for giving us an opportunity to make it right (we did eventually, after a few more months of scrambling, and at the time of writing, two years on, they're still a client). I think we're all tired of having the wool pulled over our eyes, especially in business. Be human, tell the truth, and don't try too hard to sell something. Own the flaws or faults in your product/service/business. We all have them, and it's better for you to call them out than to let somebody else do it for you.

I'M WORRIED I CAN'T MANAGE THE WORKLOAD

A lot of my more practical fears come from feeling completely overwhelmed by my workload. Sometimes I stare at my to-do list, trying to prioritise, and it feels as though I'm trying to complete a jigsaw puzzle of the sea.

I don't think it's uncommon, when we have a lot to do, to look up at our work nervously, as if from the base of a mountain. This mountain isn't part of a scenic landscape of valleys and trees, but an Excel spreadsheet with 400 rows of profit-and-loss data and an invoice discrepancy.

Just now, while writing, I looked up at my husband and said, 'I want to go swimming.' I don't have a gym membership (honestly, my idea of exercise is solo dancing in my underwear to nineties R 'n' B; it works well for me, but a few days ago I pulled my hamstring from dipping too low), it's pitch black and snowing outside, and we're in the Midlands. We're not going swimming.

'Why do you want to go swimming?' he asked.

'Because I don't want to be writing this book. I still have so long until it's finished. I keep thinking I'm getting there but I don't seem to be. I can't do it.'

I recognise this as feeling overwhelmed by the task at hand. I'm a person who's good at coming up with ideas and solutions but absolutely appalling at seeing them through (my mum calls me half-job Hulse). So writing a book is one of the most ambitious things I've ever tried to do. I feel as if I've only just developed the ability to put together a single cohesive thought. Now I have to write an entire book of them. I feel as if I have no real place writing this, and that so many others are more qualified than I am for this task. It's late and I want to go swimming. And by swimming

I actually mean watch *Free Willy* on Netflix in my pyjamas.

My husband stares at me, shrugs, and says, 'Okay. Don't write it.'

'But I want to!'

'Okay, write it.'

He knows what he's up to, this one.

The only way I can manage this fear is by tackling it with action. I've decided that I want to write the book, I've already dedicated a large number of resources to it, and the only thing that will prevent me from completing it now is me. Or *Free Willy*.

The single thing that's hindering the completion of this book is my fear that I won't be able to finish it and all efforts will have been in vain.

If you're currently reading a published version of this book, can you please spare a thought for past me, sitting at the kitchen table with straining eyes and a sore coccyx, telling myself that I can't do it.

I know that the only way I can remain positive and prevent my fear from preventing me from doing what I want is to simply keep writing the chapters and going through various edits. Writing the book is the only way to make me feel in control, and not fearful of the task at hand, no matter how momentous.

Delegating tasks or asking a team member to take some stuff off your plate can seem like a distant dream for the solitary freelancer. This need not always be the case. The ability to delegate to other freelancers while retaining quality and profit is one of the most valuable skills I've learned in the past two years (which is why I've dedicated a whole chapter to it). In a world where our time is literally our money, and we have little certainty as to whether work will keep coming in, often we just need to ship work out.

The fear that comes from a sense of overwhelming business will soon abate when you're in the midst of taking action and crossing things off your to-do list. But to take that first step onto Excel Mountain (now there's a great Disney ride!), I've found that it's critical to make positive mental associations with a task. Once I've mentally said to myself

'I don't want to do this' or 'This isn't fun', I've created a negative association with it, which makes it even harder to get the damn thing finished.

There are many specific tasks that I don't like doing, though that sense of dread I feel about completing them is largely created by me, since I make them bigger and more painful in my head (it's worth noting that if you're feeling a sense of dread about all work all the time, you should almost certainly consider a career change). Focusing on the positives that will come from completing them will help you chip through those tedious tasks. I hate writing sales proposals – I despise it – but, as I'm the owner of the business, this is what a lot of my time is taken up with. I used to put them off, or drag myself through them like a toddler leaving a theme park. Now, I find that if I focus on the excitement of a potential new client, they become much easier to complete.

When overwhelmed by your workload to the point of catatonic resistance (hello, Twitter!), don't think about everything you have to do. Just take the smallest most important thing, focus on how good it will feel when it's done, and do it. And keep doing that.

HOW WILL I PAY THE BILLS?

When you go freelance, suddenly you're responsible for generating enough money to sustain your lifestyle, and perhaps your family's. This is, objectively and rationally, bloody terrifying. But acknowledging that this has always been the case can help alleviate the pressure. A steady job is never totally secure – you could be made redundant, get fired, lose your ability to work, get usurped for a promotion, or be required to relocate. A multitude of potential circumstances means there's no such thing as an unconditional paycheque. I acknowledge, of course, that the stakes are higher when you're your own boss, but conceding that even a permanent full-time job isn't without risk will help you manage the fear of not being able to sustain yourself.

In the early days of business, when everything is new, overwhelming, and intimidating, getting a firm and clear grip on your finances is fundamental to feeling in control. This is the most obvious way to manage the fear of not being able to pay the bills, but it's often overlooked.

Many freelancers and small businesses don't understand their finances. In the first eighteen months of business, I got in such a muddle with mine. 'Muddle' being a polite word for 'total shit show'.

I've already established that admin and processes and finances aren't my forte. In fact, when I was starting out, it all actively intimidated me. There was an entire world of input VAT and sales tax that I knew nothing about, and trying to learn about it felt like climbing Everest in flip-flops, especially because I was also trying to navigate all the other psychologically crippling factors of setting up a business. Cue Monday-morning weeping.

I couldn't find the time or mental capacity to sit down and learn the intricacies of business finance. Two years later, I still haven't, though I have started to passively absorb some of it, reluctantly.

I buried my head in the sand. I would look at my bank balance and *feel* if it was healthy or not. Is there money in the bank? Is that money likely to be less than what will go out? That was the extent of my financial management – the world's worst CFO.

The absurdity of my lackadaisical approach to money becomes even more apparent when you understand that I wasn't dealing with small amounts of money. In its first year, my business turned over more than a quarter of a million pounds at a 61% profit margin (being a freelancer-only model, it has low overheads), and I managed all of this by occasionally logging in to my internet banking, looking at it for a bit, and thinking it was probably fine.

Some days I would panic because my balance was lower than normal, and I couldn't pinpoint why. I had no clear idea what was going on. I knew only that profit was being made and I was moving money around. I knew my business well in my head, but I didn't have a process or system for managing or understanding it outside of my own arbitrary measures. It doesn't exactly take an MBA to work out that this isn't good business, regardless of the size of your operation.

A real financial pitfall for a freelancer, especially if you're the single shareholder in a limited company, as I was, is suddenly having to make the distinction between 'business money' and 'my money'. I'd look at the business account and think, 'OK cool, that's my salary for a while. I'll buy a dress!' Because my business finances were healthy, I started to neglect my personal ones, and it took a solid year for me to go back to seeing my personal account as *me* and my business finances as something completely separate. When you start making income from your own efforts and this money sits in a separate account, it's hard to see it as distinct from your own finances.

In theory it's obvious, though in practice it's arduous: everyone needs to understand what they're spending, why they're spending it, and whether that spending is sensible. Not only for the glaringly obvious reason that eluded me for so long – it's important to know where your money is – but also because the process alone empowers you with a sense of control that will take that practical fear and make it, simply, practical.

Hindsight really is a glorious thing, so here's what I recommend: ensure you have a dedicated system for managing your finances that you check in with weekly. So many different tools and services are geared up to help new businesses do this. Ask your accountant what they recommend.

It's extremely important to have a good accountant – one you trust. Mine has saved me exponentially more than he costs and has taken my muddle and turned it into a clear balance sheet.

Many of the freelancers on my team choose to manage their own taxes instead of hiring an accountant. I have no real advice on this, as I think it depends entirely on the person you are, but I do think motivations are telling. If you want to manage your own taxes to get a clear handle on your finances, to understand and learn how everything works, then absolutely – enjoy and good luck! But if you're wanting to manage your own taxes only to save money, I can assure you that investing in an experienced accountant will ultimately save you more in the long run.

If you're in any way like me and break out in hives at the mention of 'financial planning', force yourself to get all of this set up and operating like a well-oiled financial machine straight away. Don't put it off, as I did. It only gets worse. Look at it in small chunks on days when you're feeling confident and in control. Slowly the habit will seep in and become second nature. I assure you, if I can do it, anyone can.

I DON'T UNDERSTAND ALL MY NEW LEGAL OBLIGATIONS

When you work for someone else, a department typically manages the business's confusing legalities and you never have to acknowledge they even exist. When you go it alone, suddenly you're faced with legal obligations that you never had before, and no amount of *Ally McBeal* binges will help you. Believe me, I've tried.

Employment law, self-assessments, contracts, NDAs – you find yourself navigating a world of legal intricacies way beyond your level of expertise.

It might not surprise you to know that I didn't have my legal ducks in a row when I first began my business. I was negotiating large global contracts based on non-disclosure agreement templates that I had downloaded, for free, from the internet.

One time, I got myself in 'a muddle' by signing a contract that actually had a completely different company name on it, which meant that the client had no legal obligation to pay me, even after the work was delivered. I'd like to say there was a sensible, adult, justifiable reason for this, but honestly, I just didn't read the contract properly. Excellent work, Kirsty. Great businessing. I managed to resolve it in the end, though the feelings of shame and frustration stayed with me for weeks. I felt like I was an idiot and didn't deserve any of the success

I'd achieved. Really, I was just inexperienced, over-worked, and overwhelmed.

It's only through our mistakes that we learn, and now, needless to say, I read all contracts – care-fully. This might seem like blindingly obvious advice, but it's amazing what slips through the cracks when we're under pressure.

As freelancers, our contracts are our only financial security, and we need to treat them with as much respect. Most of the freelancers I work with don't insist on drawing up contracts for the work we've confirmed over email. Emails can be legally binding, but there's room for disagreement here. I recom-mend removing any layer of uncertainty and setting up a small, easy-to-amend terms of service agree-ment that you can quickly edit for projects you agree to. Again, seems obvious, but few people do it.

Many online law firms (in all countries) are tailored specifically for small businesses. For a small fee, they'll draw up contracts or review them. The first thing you should do is pay the small amount to get several professional contract templates created – ones that you understand and can confidently use throughout the rest of your freelance career.

I don't think I'm experienced enough

Regardless of the market you're operating in, the freelance industry is booming. According to a report conducted by freelance recruitment site Elance (now Upwork) in 2013, the number of businesses employing freelancers increased by 46% year on year. The flexibility and high level of expertise that the freelance market can offer is worth over 21 billion pounds to the UK economy.[2] There's no shortage of talent, so to identify and secure work opportunities, you often need to act quickly.

Feeling experienced enough or knowing how to stand out in a saturated freelance marketplace can feel daunting. Understandably, you may worry that your skill set isn't as strong as the competition's, or perhaps that your development will stagnate as a result of your working alone.

You may find it reassuring to know that I've consistently found that people actually become better at their jobs the longer they freelance. I think this is because when you work in a large business, you

---

[2] www.csd.org.uk/content/uploads/2015/07/gen-y-and-the-gigging-economy.pdf

can hide your failures behind your boss or the company, or you can ask others to complete a task for you rather than learn how to do it yourself. When I was working in a large agency and made a mistake, I would rarely personally address it. I had one of those great bosses who acknowledged that her teams' failures were also hers, so she would help rectify the mistakes I made. Likewise, I worked alongside literally hundreds of smart people, so fell into the trap of asking someone to do a task for me if it sat even slightly outside of my direct area of expertise. If there's nobody else to rely on or ask for help, or if the buck stops with you if anything goes wrong, you have to pull yourself up by your bootstraps, fill any gaps in your knowledge, and address issues head-on, independently.

This might sound intimidating, but it actually presents a huge opportunity. Use your new-found freedom to spend some time honing your skills or learning new ones. Join networks and groups within your industry to ensure that you remain ahead of the curve. Working for yourself can mean that you don't have people sat at the desk next to you to learn from, and nobody to compare yourself against to make sure you're not falling behind. Create this for yourself by speaking with other freelancers and industry peers.

If you're fearful that you won't be experienced enough to stand out from the competition, take that fear and use it to hone your skill set. We're fortunate enough to be living in a collaborative age with numerous opportunities for knowledge- and skills-sharing in both the digital and real world. Find your space in these worlds and take the opportunity to own your development. Learn new skills and improve on your current ones in ways that suit you.

I DON'T WANT TO FEEL LIKE AN AMATEUR

This is a fear that few can admit to but many feel, including me. As we work our way up in our careers, we start to understand what's going on day-to-day, earn respect from our peers, and feel senior and established. It's incredibly difficult to walk away from that and go back to a place of uncertainty. But I implore you to let go of the sense of pride you get from being experienced and certain and to focus instead on the contentment you can get from doing something you truly enjoy, or working in the way you want to work. This contentment can quickly overshadow the ego that tells us it's better to remain accomplished.

CHAPTER FOUR
REMEMBERING TO GET DRESSED

'Always remember to put on shoes.' This was one of the first bits of advice I received on being my own boss, managing my own schedule, and working from home, and it came from my good friend Oli. He'd gone freelance about a year before me so was well versed in these apparent necessities. Oli believes that putting on shoes makes you feel as though you're going somewhere and doing something, regardless of whether you are or not. He works alone from his basement, so I can only assume that he smartly ties his best brogues and walks into his dark and dingy basement office to tinker with code and listen to thrash metal all day. Honestly, there are far worse ways to live.

When I first went freelance, I didn't do this. I did the opposite. I was living alone and working alone; my life wasn't subject to peer review, and I could conduct myself without fear of judgement or criticism. For a woman who enjoys camping primarily because it means I can legitimately avoid showers, this was dangerous territory.

If I had lots of tasks I needed to execute, rather than client meetings or calls, I'd typically fall asleep with my laptop by my bed at night. The moment my alarm went off in the morning, I'd sit up, pick up my laptop, and get straight into it. I wouldn't let myself get out of bed, even for a coffee, until I'd finished what I needed to finish – a tactic I'd developed at university. This certainly meant that I got a lot of stuff done, normally before 10am, no less, but it also meant that my life was a fairly mirthless existence.

Those small moments that give days a pleasing aesthetic – a good breakfast, morning exercise, *fresh air* – had been replaced with vacant productivity. I don't believe that working in your pyjamas from bed on the odd occasion is detrimental to your wellbeing or productivity. But my experience suggests that doing this every day, and building it into your routine, results in linking your productivity to your sense of self-worth. And this is detrimental to your wellbeing. The more I lived to deliver work, the more difficult I found it to manage the stresses of being your own boss because I had no distractions and few little joys. When your day-to-day routine is consumed by work, it's virtually impossible to do anything other than get bogged down in it. This wasn't exactly the pleasing work–life balance I'd wanted when I decided to go it alone.

After a solid six months of not remembering to get dressed, right before my human skin was to be replaced with sweatpants and a hoodie, I heeded my friend's advice and put on shoes. And in terms of my emotional wellbeing, it was surprisingly transformative. The catalyst for this was a creeping sense that I was losing myself. Many of us express our identities through getting ready in the morning. When I fall into a reverie about, oh, accepting a BAFTA or sunning myself on a beach, I'm never, interestingly enough, doing this in my pyjamas with messy hair and makeup running down my face. We have an idea of ourselves that represents what we look like 'ready'. I'd stopped investing time in getting ready, so I ultimately stopped feeling ready.

Now, I put shoes on every single day to 'go to work' (walk into the other room). Oli was right – there's something about walking around in your bare feet that makes you feel lackadaisical. I'm an adult, and as much as I want to, I'm not going to totter round the house in just my knickers and a T-shirt anymore. I have serious business to do, and for this, I need a routine.

Many freelancers decide to find an office space so they can maintain the distinction between work life and home life and stick to their usual office hours routine. Most cities also have good and affordable co-working spaces. I've tried them, but they've never worked for me personally. I find being around many people but not working with any of them directly a little isolating. I also adore not having to commute, and the extra time that having an office in my home affords me. I'm generally more productive in the mornings, so getting up early and getting straight to it (after physically getting out of bed and getting dressed nowadays, in my developed business adulthood) works well for me.

Self-preservation

When you first start, freelancing can be lonely, and this can result in your focusing primarily on work. Without those small positive distractions that happen in a busy office environment, such as a co-worker playing a prank or your team enjoying lunch together, you might feel a little suffocated. But I've discovered many ways to mitigate the isolation and loneliness of freelancing. Here are a few of them.

Eat

One of the real joys of working from home is you suddenly have a world of slow, indulgent breakfast opportunities in front of you. When I was working in offices, breakfast would either be a rushed dry granola bar on the bus, or cereal dripping down my chin while getting through emails at my desk. Or, it would be skipped entirely.

Now, however, I give myself at least fifteen minutes (often more – fifteen minutes is a happy minimum) every morning to make and eat breakfast. Having learned from my mistakes, I now avoid the temptation to read emails or make calls while eating. I've found that approaching the day with this moment of quiet and still, just for me, creates a much calmer working environment throughout the rest of the day. The simple but definitive act of putting your personal needs before the business's goes a long way to prevent that common trap of being defined by work. If you feel as though you're largely defined by your professional life, and it controls you rather than you it, try making some time in the morning just for you, before anything else, to see if you can slowly start to remember that you're an individual outside of your email signature.

When you have TF tapping you on the shoulder from the moment you wake up, urging you to get going and make the most of your day, taking the time to slow down and ease into the day is essential.

CALL, DON'T EMAIL

As mentioned, freelancing can be quite lonely, particularly in the first few months, while you're adjusting to working alone. This is what most people tell to me when they talk about their experience transitioning from working in an office environment to working for themselves, alone. I don't want to sound like my CV here, but I really *do* thrive in a team environment. There are days when I miss the routine and regularity of working in an office. I miss the energy and positivity that you can get from working with people in a lively environment.

About three months into working from home, I got into a dangerous habit of solo afternoon karaoke. Let me repeat that. Solo. Afternoon. Karaoke. Just to *hear something* and break the monotony of solitude. I hadn't quite adjusted at that point, and I felt isolated and overwhelmed (though I did get very good at 'Midnight Train to Georgia', so, silver lining).

A little trick to break the silence is to stop relying exclusively on instant messaging or email for communication. Picking up the phone and actually speaking to someone can have a huge impact on your day. And if the people you call are freelance, it's likely they'll appreciate it, too.

Have a regular lunch or coffee shop

Going to a coffee shop or cafe regularly can be an ideal way to break up your day and indulge in some important socialising. Make friends with your local barista, and pop in whenever you need a break from work, or in those moments when you're at risk of a solo afternoon karaoke binge. We freelancers lack the casual water-cooler chat, so we need to create it for ourselves. Going to the gym is also a good way to break up your day and interact with other people, but I wouldn't know about that.

CREATE A WORKSPACE

I spent the better part of a year working from the kitchen table or the sofa. I was so afraid of failure at the time that you could have sat me on a washing line and I would have delivered a thirty-page presentation (though this really isn't the easiest way to focus). Living in London, the thought of a dedicated home office feels like an indulgence quite out of my reach, but I have created a dedicated workspace: a desk in the corner facing the window. Set boundaries so that people cannot distract you when you're in this space, and try to avoid doing anything else there. Reserve your online shopping and YouTube videos on how to get the perfect eyebrow arch for elsewhere in the home.

And if you don't want to commit to a full-time desk space or a permanent office space but sometimes enjoy a space with reliable Wi-Fi and people to talk to, check out sites such as Spacehop (www.spacehop. com) and Deskcamping (www.deskcamping.com), where people let their homes or offices for the day at affordable rates.

Join groups and spend too much time on Twitter

Whatever industry or market you work in, you'll always be able to find other freelancers and independents to engage with, whether in real life at meetups and networking events or online on social media platforms such as LinkedIn and Twitter. I found Twitter to be invaluable in the early lonely days of freelancing. You can have conversations with experts in your field, get help on issues, and find people to collaborate with. I've also found that asking other freelancers to go for coffee or to work together in someone's home is well received. The great thing about freelancing is that nearly all freelancers are in the same boat when it comes to loneliness – so use social media to find and reach out to others. It can be a great way to recreate what you miss about a busy office environment. You just need to tread a fine line between being social and managing procrastination.

MANAGING PROCRASTINATION

When you first go freelance, you might revert to your state of nature. State of nature (mentioned here to make use of my impotent philosophy degree) is a concept used in moral and political philosophy. It describes the hypothetical conditions of people's lives before formal societies existed. To poorly paraphrase the seventeenth-century philosopher Thomas Hobbes, in the state of nature, without the framework of society, man becomes the worst version of himself. When you first become your own boss, for perhaps the first time in your life (maybe second, if you went to university), you're completely in control of how, and where, you spend your day. Without the framework of angry bosses and structured commutes, it can sometimes be a struggle to adjust to working without slipping into our state of nature. It's really only my practical fears that prevent me from behaving like Macaulay Culkin when he checks into the Four Seasons – all I want to do is sit in my living room and charge ice cream and buckets of M&Ms to my dad's credit card.

When I first became a freelancer, I declared to myself, and to some suffering friends, that I would 'never set an alarm again'. Oh, how naive I was. I did this for a while; I got up when I woke up, and listened to my own circadian rhythm, *man*. But I soon found myself with meetings, calls, and deadlines that forced me back to the early-morning routine I'd hoped to escape.

Self-motivation is one of the key challenges of being freelance, particularly if you're like me and sit on the lazier end on the initiative spectrum. People often don't believe me when I say I'm lazy – 'but you do so much!' But I am naturally lazy. In any given situation, I would nearly always rather be napping or eating (who wouldn't?). I've simply learned to mitigate this by tapping into TF. When I feel like things are going well and there's no pressure, you can't see me for dust.

Many of my freelance friends report that their homes are *so clean*. All the chores get done, and laundry is washed faster than it can be created. I can vouch for this, too. I'd never been a tidy person (my bedroom often looked as if it could be shortlisted for the Turner Prize), but suddenly, out of nowhere, I began tidying it. Every day.

This is nothing more than good old procrastination. And though it's not at all unique to the freelance world, when you work from home, or act as master of your day, it can be incredibly difficult to stay focused.

This is exactly where practical fears can be motivating. Nothing will put a fire in your belly like the fear of not being able to pay your rent next month. Tapping into TF is my tried-and-tested method of managing the lure of procrastination. That said, you need to feel TF in a way that's motivating, not overly stressful or debilitating.

I find it hugely helpful to write out my tasks for the day and assign them a time. For example: 8 – 9, check emails, 9 – 11, work on a presentation, etc. Keep gaps in the schedule for the inevitable client crisis or urgent request so that it's wholly realistic to stick to. A schedule will provide you with regular checkpoints, and therefore, the opportunity to see how much you're procrastinating. It will also give you something visceral and real to refer to.

I've tried to use Trello and other digital equivalents to create schedules, but they don't work for me. The act of writing down my tasks first thing in the morning, so that they stare back at me throughout the day, is the best way for me to stay productive. If you stray, think about *why* you wrote those things down and tap into TF of not finishing them – that should keep you on track. And the great thing is, the best way to manage TF is to just do your work. When I stick to a schedule rigorously, I nearly always end my day feeling accomplished.

CHAPTER FIVE
LEARNING TO SWITCH OFF

Today, as I was writing this, my dad had a severe stroke. He currently cannot speak and has no recollection of his wife of forty years and his five adult children. When the consultant asked him how old he was, he turned to my mum and said, 'We've lived there for a while, I think?'

It's interesting to note that as I sit in my bedroom contemplating what all this means for my family, I've decided to be productive and write this chapter of my book. There are a couple of reasons for this. Firstly, as a freelancer, regardless of the circumstances, it's so difficult to take time off without feeling guilty about not doing enough, or being productive enough. I feel this guilt on most days, and today I've learned that I feel it even on the darkest of days. Secondly, sometimes it just feels good to take something sad and turn it into something useful. So, here we are.

I spent most of today talking to my family and secretly crying in the shower (that famous British reserve again!). Now, I'm drinking wine and writing. I've not worked today, and despite the circumstances, this doesn't make me feel good. Not at all. In fact, as mentioned, it makes me feel guilty. Despite the circumstances, I'm still struggling to justify my decision to put work on the back burner, just for today. Conversely, I know that if I were still traditionally employed, I would have taken the day off and not thought twice about it.

My life's goalposts have changed. Now, it's not so easy to deprioritise my workload. Now, TF tells me that deprioritising my workload, even for one day, is deprioritising my clients, who allow me to generate revenue, or my team, the people who allow my business to function.

I thought that over the past two years I'd got significantly better at switching off and not letting guilt and fear prevent me from taking care of myself and my family first and foremost. Today has been valuable and illuminating in that sense. This chapter, which was supposed to be about the lessons I learned in the past, must now be about a business owner who still needs to learn how to switch off. It would be completely disingenuous of me to focus on the things I do to help me breeze through a life without worry. Instead, I'll focus on the emotional difficulties that freelancing can bring, and how we can try to combat them to maintain a healthy work–life balance, despite that very real difficulty of switching off, even on the hardest days of our lives.

I think the first step to getting better at managing crushing freelancer guilt is to simply admit its existence. It's not something we talk about much. We live in a world where stress often represents ambition and drive, and in a world where we see others' lives through what they choose to share on social media. I'll share client wins, images of the snazzy meeting room I hire infrequently, or a status about how great my team members are. I don't, however, share the moments when I'm struggling to get out of bed because I feel crushed by the weight of responsibility, or when clients are unhappy, or when the team let me down and I'm wondering why I'm even bothering at all.

THE TWO PIECES OF ADVICE

As business owners, and people in general, we are repeatedly given two hugely distinct pieces of advice. We are told to take care of ourselves, to take things slowly, to not put too much pressure on ourselves, and to understand the value of what's important in life (that is, family, friends, and love). And in the same breath, we are told to push ourselves, to hustle, to work harder than the competition, and to strive for success, often at any cost.

A specific example of this second piece of advice springs to mind. Just before Christmas, the CEO of a huge corporation tweeted that the holiday time is when those people who really deserve success will take the opportunity to work when their competitors are not, to see the holiday period as a chance to get a head start on productivity. This tweet, that ultimately suggested taking a break means you don't deserve success, got thousands of retweets, suggesting to thousands upon thousands of people that rest is weakness.

We live in an 'entrepreneurs' hustle' culture, where many famous business influencers advocate sixteen-hour days, sleeping less, and working weekends. If you're stressed, if you're busy, if you're working more than everybody else around you, you're hustling, succeeding, winning – this is the message. These entrepreneurs, who are role models for many, rarely say, 'This is psychologically exhausting; remember to rest.' There's no acknowledgement of that reality, only the constant idealisation of busyness. Working hard is rewarding, and essential to achieving success, without question. But success shouldn't come at the cost of routinely switching off and taking it easy.

At the start-up events I've attended, the focus is typically on how to stay productive, how to get your morning routine down and get up at dawn, and how to stay motivated to consistently deliver a high level of output. In isolation, these things don't allow us to be kind to ourselves. We do need to talk about all of these things as business owners, of course, but we also need to be talking about rest.

Working for yourself, particularly when you first start, is psychologically exhausting. When you go freelance, you will most likely feel a perpetual pressure to work hard, all the time. You will likely feel that if you don't, it will all fall apart.

The weight of responsibility is a burden that can sometimes, *sometimes*, outweigh the freedom and flexibility that being your own boss affords. Bosses are legally obliged to encourage you to take a break and switch off from the responsibilities that your employment entails. I am my boss, and she runs this ship like a turn-of-the-century mill owner.

I've just started to learn how to switch off and not check my phone or fear a phone call when I take a day for myself. And I've figured out how to do this on my own because most business advice available encourages the opposite.

You'll likely be surrounded by business content that tells you to push yourself, to do something that scares you – content that tells you success lies only at the end of your comfort zone. But you may also see general content that tells you to look after yourself, engage in self-care, eat well, exercise, get enough rest, and be mindful.

These two sentiments (love yourself vs. push yourself) form the core of every piece of advice I've ever given or received. If you think back, you'll probably realise this is the case for you, too. We dole them out or accept them interchangeably, depending on the person/scenario/situation. But really, *which one should we choose?*

Can we do both? In an overarching theoretical way, yes. It seems sensible to say that sometimes we need a boost, whereas other times we need comfort, and these pieces of advice help us achieve our best within our ever-changing circumstances.

But practically, day-to-day, when we have decisions to make or challenges to face, if we don't give preference to one over the other, how do we stop them from fighting for our attention? How do we decide when to accept our vulnerability and when to force ourselves to do something excruciating? I think most of us ramble through our lives awkwardly juggling both. Displaying the polarised symptoms of living in a world that tells us to take it easy and smash all barriers at exactly the same time, we follow a fifty-hour work week with a forty-two-hour Netflix binge.

The way to mitigate this is to try not to pressure ourselves to live life in the extreme. We don't necessarily need to work a sixteen-hour day to be successful, and we don't necessarily need to spend an entire day on the sofa to feel rested. We need to find our own rhythm to establish a work life that's balanced and sustainable.

It took me about eighteen months to feel confident enough to take my first, glorious day off during the week. By day off, I don't mean a day off-ish. I'd grown accustomed to days off-ish. These are the 'I'll just quickly send this email then do a call this afternoon' days off. Or the 'I'll fly to a different time zone and get up at 5.30am to do some calls then maybe take the afternoon to feel guilty' days off. I'm talking about the kind of day off where you're not even thinking about work, where it's no longer your responsibility. You've put your out-of-office and sun cream on, and it's your time to relax and do nothing. Or, more accurately, think nothing and worry nothing. It's your time to step away from work without the fear and guilt that can hover like a cloud. I'm now in a much healthier position – I can take regular breaks when I need them to fully switch off. It did take time to get to this point, and I took certain steps to get here.

ACHIEVING BALANCE

Ultimately, we all need to remember to balance work, play, and rest. How we do this is entirely subjective, but this is what has helped me begin to achieve that balance over the past couple of years.

REMEMBER THAT A SMALL BREAK IS BETTER THAN NO BREAK AT ALL

For me, the thought of taking a full week off is too daunting. Victorian-mill-owner Kirsty just won't have it. One day I will, but I'm not there yet. I started by taking an afternoon off here and there, and then a day. Small breaks to completely switch off are still valuable and will allow you to adjust and learn that it's OK, everything won't burst into flames the moment you disconnect from Wi-Fi. Like anything else in business, rest is something we need to learn how to do, and starting small and enjoying small chunks of rest at a time is one way we can create that all-important balance.

Spend downtime doing things you actually want to do

Weekends and evenings often get quickly filled with social obligations. Unless you really, really want to do something, say no. Honestly, nobody displays greater resolve and resourcefulness than I do when it comes to getting out of weekend plans. When you're pushing yourself hard, you'll probably find you just want to spend days and evenings switching your brain off in isolation. You'll get FOMO (fear of missing out), you'll annoy a few acquaintances, but those important to you will understand. In becoming your own boss, you've already taken on a lot of additional pressure and likely a heavy workload alongside it, so absolve yourself of the societal pressure to be at every event or gathering. Accept that there will be days when you cancel last minute. Accept that you can't be everywhere and go to everything. Accept that you may lose a few casual friendships along the way. Those friendships that aren't solely reliant on an evening in the pub will remain.

MEDITATE

Yes, it's a cliché and no, it doesn't necessarily involve wearing a tunic, but it does help. Just ten minutes of meditation can be hugely reinvigorating when you're starting to burn out. The Headspace app is a good start. I prefer to use guided meditations on YouTube because you can pick them according to your mood.

NAP

When I first started Manyminds, I got into the habit of taking twenty-minute afternoon naps. I find it's just enough to reset myself when I feel stress creep in. I tend to have huge afternoon slumps, where I struggle to concentrate and focus. Instead of forcing myself to push through this, or caffeinating myself until my hands shake, I allow myself this small amount of time to recharge and refocus. For me, napping is like cheating at meditation.

TRY WORKING WEEKENDS TO TAKE A WEEKDAY OFF

I like working on Sundays – there's less pressure, fewer phone calls, no meetings. I can get up later, have a coffee, and focus for a few hours. If you're really struggling with your workload but feel you need a break, get work done during the weekend and take the Monday off. You'll still get your work done, but in a less pressurised situation, and you'll get used to not always being on during the week. (I think this is pretty much the only way I remained relatively sane during year one.)

Keep things in perspective

It's easy to let your business define you and to take business failures personally. In the early days, when my focus was almost exclusively on the business, it was so hard to switch off from it and not take business mistakes or bad days personally, as there was little else to divert my attention to.

Around the time I started the business, I also decided to pursue a lifelong whimsy of becoming a stand-up comedian. Humour and not taking myself too seriously is, and likely always will be, my armour. Within weeks of winning my first contract, I sat down at my kitchen table, Googled 'open mic stand-up London' and signed up without giving myself the chance to protest. I dragged along two of my closest and ever-supportive friends and got blind drunk. The organisers pulled names out of a hat, so I had no idea where on the bill I'd be among twenty-two acts. Bad luck would have it that I was the twenty-second name pulled, so by the time it came to my turn, I'd been drowning my nerves for a good couple of hours. I got on the stage, told some jokes, and to my utter delight and surprise, made some kind and welcoming strangers laugh. Pumped up with bad merlot and adrenaline, at the end of my set I fell off the stage, crashed in to the front row and stumbled into my seat.

I was hooked. I started gigging two or three times a week and even went to the expense and effort of doing a run at the Edinburgh Fringe. A lot of my friends thought I was absolutely bonkers for taking on so much at once, but the stand-up comedy provided the distraction I needed. If I was stressed about work, which I perpetually was, I could step away and write some jokes, or do a gig and enjoy something else – something that was just for me. The comedy was crucial for my being able to switch off and let my mind focus on something else for a while.

Running an agency of independents who are all business owners in their own right, I've found that those with children typically tend to be a little better at switching off from work. I think because they have something much greater to focus on. If you don't have children or other significant responsibilities, find something meaningful to you outside of your business that will allow you to keep things in perspective. This will prevent you from becoming defined by your business performance.

Create a safety net

This is the most obvious tactic but the hardest one to implement. Create a safety net of people who can run things in your absence. I struggled with this for a long time, not necessarily because I'm bad at delegating, but because one of the biggest challenges of being a business owner is avoiding being the exclusive face of your business. If you can avoid this, you have a business that scales and a weeklong break with your name on it. For those of you who often work alone and struggle to find people to delegate to while retaining a profit, there's a whole chapter on this later in the book.

Don't worry about what your competitors are doing

Focusing on the competition can be a damaging distraction. Run your business in a way that works for you and allows you to be the best version of yourself.

There is a temptation, of course, to get wrapped up in how much effort your peers are putting in, or how successful they are, or how long they work. While it may be strategically beneficial to have an eye on your competitive landscape, don't find yourself defining your own performance by those of others. Focus on your own work and output first and foremost.

Overall, we're all human, we all get overwhelmed, we all need rest. There's no merit in working yourself to the point of being useless to those around you (I speak from experience here). And, honestly, that probably means not working sixteen-hour days.

Ultimately, we need to work hard to be successful. But it's equally important to rest well to be successful. Strive for balance, to get to a point where you're productive without feeling stressed or overwhelmed. Work the number of hours that allows you to achieve this balance. They say that what makes the world's greatest wines is the harmony of the key elements – no element sticks out more than another. We need to be like great wine.

As I adjust to feeling less stressed out about work, I sometimes find myself interpreting this negatively. I think that maybe that I'm not working hard enough or don't care enough, but this isn't the case. Try to remember that balance, not panic, stress, or busyness, is the marker of drive and ambition.

CHAPTER SIX
FAILING FAST

We all make mistakes. And sometimes we make absolute doozies. Obviously, many of the mistakes we make are a result of not knowing what we're doing, and as we navigate through life, we (hopefully) make fewer mistakes as a result of our experiences. When I first started running a business, I was, what they call in the professional world, an absolute shitshow.

I made so many mistakes, constantly. Perhaps no greater, though, than electing to casually give away 50% of my business (no buy-in requirement) to a relative stranger. Fortunately, this relative stranger also turned out to be an excellent human, so it all worked out amicably in the end.

The reason I made this absolute doozie of a mistake was simply a lack of confidence in my ability to remain solvent and stable on my own. My now close friend said to me, as we walked through a park in New York just after I'd set up alone, 'I think I'm going to start doing my own thing and work with freelancers, just like you.' Rather than coming to the reasonable conclusion of 'Cool, there's plenty of work to go round', my mind, in its vulnerable state, said, 'NO. That will completely ruin all my chances of success, and everything I've done so far will be a waste of my time and I'll be left in the gutter humiliated and alone.'

At the time, I hadn't yet had any real success in the business. I had nothing to fall back on to give me confidence in my abilities. I simply wasn't able to make considered, rational decisions. I was insecure and afraid of failing. And so, in a state of panic, I just blurted out loud, 'Why don't you just join me? Here! Own half of my [already profitable, scaled, and successful] business! TAKE IT!'

I'm as embarrassed admitting this as I'm sure you are reading it.

We had both just started out, and were each running our own profitable businesses. Looking back, we effectively managed to convince ourselves for a good few weeks that this was a sensible decision. There were shareholder agreements, which I didn't read or understand, there were business dates with wine and dinner (they were nice), and there were conversations about future growth during which my stomach churned and smashed against my sides in an attempt to make me notice this wasn't right for my business, and probably not hers either. As my new friend and I started to work together, it became increasingly apparent that we wanted very different things from the business – different projects, different clients, and different areas of focus.

Lisa is a woman in my industry whom I respect greatly. I tried to work for her once, and she didn't hire me on account of having a hunch that I'd run my own company one day. I'm still astounded that during an hour-long meeting, she saw something in me that I hadn't seen in all my life. During my partnership days, we were at a conference together in Valencia, and one evening she took me aside and said, 'I'm surprised to see you in this partnership. You can do this on your own, you know. You don't need someone else.' Given that she'd elucidated my entire existence with her perception once, I decided to really take note this time, and with a sinking feeling, I started thinking about how to wriggle my way out of the partnership. A new company had been formed, documents had been signed. We were very sensible in the execution of it all, looking back (that was definitely her, not me), but, how exactly *does* one unsign a shareholder agreement weeks after initially signing it?

I spent days tormented over how to broach this conversation and cause as little offence as possible. I'd grown to like and respect my partner very much. I just knew the decision for us to go into business together hadn't been right, for either of us. I planned out the exact phrasing and made the exasperatingly belated but sensible decision to get legal advice. Then, after days of planning exactly what to say in a constructive face-to-face meeting, I found myself just pouring my heart out on the phone to her while browsing the Two Can Dine for £10 section in M&S.

'I don't think we should have the business partner-ship anymore.'

I was expecting to get into messy legal negotiations. I acknowledged that the mistake was all on me, that there was nobody else to blame, and that I had to rectify it however necessary, and as swiftly and fairly as possible. I wanted to salvage the friendship first and foremost, though I understood that given the circumstances, salvaging the friendship might be tricky. To my delight and relief, it turned out that I hadn't been the only party reconsidering the rushed and naive decision to enter into a partnership, and we resolved everything by simply signing the business back to me and agreeing to work together and support each other as much as possible in the future. I'd never felt so acutely aware that being nice is the most important thing in business.

The reason this ended so amicably, however, was that I didn't sit in my mistake; I acknowledged it and moved on – quickly. The longer I'd waited on this one, the worse it would have got.

About 90% of the tens of freelancers I know and have worked with over the past decade or so say that they went through the 'blindly saying yes to everything' phase. When we start up, if work is offered to us, we're certainly going to take it, and we'll likely overpromise, or set deadlines that leave us staying up until 3am high on Haribo and cheap wine doing technical audits. This mistake comes from a lack of confidence in our ability to keep and retain work. We say yes to whatever we can get, and go out of way to keep our clients, suppliers, or users happy, meaning we risk under-delivering and not meeting expectations. If you are yet to go freelance, I don't want you to beat yourself up when you do this – it happens to the best of us, and it's a crucial lesson in working out your own time-management system. Taking on too much and overpromising in the beginning is a path many freelancers go down in the early days. Ultimately, we learn exactly what we can realistically achieve and how. We shouldn't focus on the mistake, but on how to stop making it.

Learning to fix mistakes

My learning how to fix mistakes quickly is perhaps the primary reason that my business is profitable today. For six or so months, it wasn't a profitable business, and I went into alarming personal debt to fund it. I always paid my freelancers on time, regardless of whether I was getting paid or not. Many of you may discover that as a new business with no credit history or ability to prove income, it's actually difficult to get into business debt. I simply didn't have the time to raise capital (that whole global airline as my first client thing), I had no personal capital or family money, and the bank didn't want to give me a penny, so personal debt and bootstrapping it was.

As an aside, this inability to get funding and go into business debt is now something for which I'm incredibly grateful. I always encourage people to avoid it if they possibly can. I was able to pivot and change and constantly evolve autonomously, and crucially, I was able to make mistakes without significant financial repercussions. If you're selling a service, as I am, as opposed to building a product, you're likely to be in a better position to avoid going into business debt.

The primary reason for my business's negative profit in the first few months was cash flow. Every small business's nightmare. You have staff (in my case, freelancers) to keep happy and bills to pay, and to do this, you have to wait for other businesses to pay you, and this never seems to happen as promptly or regularly as promised. People pay late – accept it and prepare for it and build it into your cash-flow model so it doesn't get you in a muddle later down the line.

The second reason was that working with multiple freelancers, for the first time, meant that I was often paying for work three or four times. For example, I would charge a client for five days of work (with a mark-up that covered the freelancer's fee) and then source a freelancer to complete it. This only works, of course, if in fact five days of work are required to complete the project. Some freelancers are inevitably better than others, and until I had the chance to work with each one once, I didn't know whether their work would be good enough. Before I'd managed to build up my network of tried-and-tested, reliable freelancers, I would give a freelancer the project, discover the work wasn't good enough (or couldn't be delivered on time), and then have to find someone else, immediately, to step in.

This was quite problematic at first. The only way to manage this problem was to quickly work out which freelancers were worth working with. This was a hard reality, as I had to let people down, and take projects from freelancers if they didn't deliver. I wasn't left with much room for patience or generosity. I had to be ruthless. I couldn't give people limitless chances or risk driving my businesses into the ground paying people who weren't up to scratch. I found this excruciating. I wanted to create an inclusive environment in which people could try and fail and thrive. I wanted to let people let me down and give them the benefit of the doubt. I did this for a long time, and it resulted in significant losses that I still pay for personally, literally, and metaphorically today. Once more, I found myself having to learn, quickly, that any mistakes within my business were ultimately my mistakes. I had to learn, quickly, that if I made the mistake of not choosing my team correctly, I had to rectify it. This often looked like scrambling about getting recommendations from peers or old colleagues, and on occasion it meant delivering work late and upsetting our clients.

DEALING WITH UNHAPPY CLIENTS

Over the last two years, my clients have generally been very happy. For the first eighteen months or so, I never lost a client, never had to settle a dispute, and never experienced that awful moment of picking up the phone to talk through a project I delivered badly. My relationships with clients were positive. They were always happy with the work, and I was always proud of it. I genuinely thought I'd solved the agency problem and that was that. My clients were happy and always would be.

Until recently.

Recently, for the first time, Manyminds had a very unhappy client. It wasn't entirely my fault, the client wasn't entirely unjustified, but it did leave me feeling entirely hopeless.

I worked in agencies for years, so I know all too well that unhappy clients are a commonplace reality of the supplier–agency dynamic. I spent the better part of my career managing this. Here's one particularly delightful scenario. I'd been employed to manage a team in an agency, and on my very first day, at ten in the morning, when I'd barely had the chance to sign in to Outlook, I was told that I had a meeting with a dissatisfied client and it was my job to convince her to stay with the agency. Nothing like a good baptism of fire to get a working relationship started.

I was used to unhappy clients, but it was a different story the first time it had happened in *my* company, on *my* watch. I'd wanted so desperately for Manyminds to be different and to not have these conversations with clients. I struggled to view the situation as an objective reality of running a marketing agency.

What happened was my team and I had spent a lot of time and effort creating a London-centric campaign, and two days later, devastating and tragic attacks happened in London. Overnight, our jolly, optimistic, tongue-in-cheek London-centric marketing campaign that we'd spent weeks pulling together fell apart, and our client had spent money on a campaign that we couldn't so much as tweet. I told the client we would park it for now and revisit it later, once the dust had settled. This ended up being a mistake, as I ultimately just delayed the difficult conversation instead of addressing it head-on. After this, another campaign for the same client flopped, to everyone's surprise and disappointment. We desperately tried to change angles, find new audiences to engage, but the money had already been spent and we were increasingly aware that we were losing time, energy, effort, and resources on activity that wasn't driving returns. We had to hold up our hands and wave our white flag. We couldn't win this one.

To be fair, the results weren't terrible, but they weren't what we'd hoped for. They were just OK. They were resolutely mediocre, and mediocrity isn't exactly what I'd sold.

We didn't effectively communicate the effort we'd put in, and our mediocre performance left the client feeling as though we were just another indifferent, mediocre agency, and they were unhappy with the overall experience.

This makes me terribly sad. Not a 'nine-to-five go home and have a glass of wine and forget about it' sad, but the sad that comes from a *personal* failure because *your* business hasn't met expectations.

There's an unfortunate grey area in our industry where we can agree on output and deliver against that but if our output doesn't yield expected returns, where does the responsibility lie?

In this particular instance, it lay somewhere in the middle. We'd been paid for a service we only partially delivered, but it cost me and my business the agreed amount. There's an understanding that uncontrollable variables can lead to a lack of guarantees in any marketing or advertising campaign, but still, this didn't change the reality that money seemed to be wasted, trust was lost, and no party went away feeling satisfied – kind of like a bad date.

This was the first time I had this experience as a business owner, it has happened since, and I'm sure it will happen again, but there are some lessons from the first experience I take with me now.

1. Communicate when things aren't going to plan – even if you think you can turn it round and solve whatever problem you're currently having, transparency always wins.

2. Agree on what constitutes failure in advance. This may not seem like the most positive way to start a relationship, but set clear boundaries and goals right away, as grey areas can make resolutions messy.

3. Have as many projects as possible on the go at the same time, to mitigate the impact of unexpected failure. If one project doesn't go as expected, then it's less problematic if there are also other things happening. Never put all your eggs in one basket, as they say.

Finally, own your mistakes. Not everything we do is going to be a great success, and the sooner we can all start admitting that to ourselves, and our clients, and our industry peers, the better we'll all get at managing, and preventing, mistakes.

It has been advantageous to acknowledge every one of my mistakes as a freelancer to date and then move on *as quickly as possible*. It's all too easy to sit in them, fear the difficult conversations, or think if we just ignore them they'll go away.

It's crucial to listen to your instincts. If something just doesn't feel quite right but you can't put your finger on exactly why, then just trust it's not right. Our instincts are the manifestation of our subconscious mind working incredibly quickly, processing information we've not yet had time to rationalise. In our busy and distracted lives, our instinct is a powerful tool to prevent mistakes that should not be ignored. Listen to your gut and focus on moving forwards.

CHAPTER SEVEN
WORKING WITH FREELANCERS AND REMOTE TEAMS

Since I run a business that relies exclusively on freelance resource, I've developed a pool of reliable freelancers to draw on. This took a lot of trial and error, and the biggest takeaway – from a long series of poor choices when it came to whom I worked with and how – was that I became adept at quickly determining which freelancers are good ones, and which ones are not.

Through my mistakes, I'm now armed with a good understanding of how to efficiently access the infinitely scalable global freelance talent pool. As we increasingly move into a world where remote working is commonplace for both the self-employed and the employed, this skill has proven invaluable.

You may be a business owner or manager who's looking to expand and take on new opportunities, or you may be a freelancer in the fortunate position of having more work than you can do, desperate to ship it to someone else. You may be employed but think you'd enjoy working remotely, or you may be an employer who'd like to allow your staff to work from home. Whatever your current situation, working with freelancers and remote teams has significant benefits for all parties. The business that chooses to work with freelancers or remote teams has the benefit of an unlimited talent pool. Traditionally, businesses have been limited to hiring people within a thirty-mile radius, but if you work with freelancers, suddenly you have access to a world of talent at your fingertips. Remote working also provides the benefit of low overheads, meaning, of course, higher profits.

First, however, the most important thing to remember when building a freelancer team is to ensure that your freelancers are *actually freelance*. As in highly publicised cases such as Uber, some companies work with people on a self-employed basis when they act more like an employee, meaning they deserve all the associated rights. Any freelancer you work with should have a freelance career, and clients, outside of your business. They should not derive all of their wage from you and should be completely autonomous with their time, how they work and the projects they choose to work on. If your freelance team could not individually sustain their freelance careers without your single projects, it is perhaps more beneficial to consider them employees. Otherwise, if they are independent, successful business owners in their own right, then choosing to work with freelancers can provide a wealth of benefits for all involved.

Aside from the financial benefits, working with an exclusively freelance team can have societal benefits as well. There are many reasons for this, but the first is both simple and well documented. According to the *World Happiness Report 2017*, 'Being self-employed tends to be associated with higher life evaluation and positive affect (as compared to being a full-time employee) across Europe, North America, Australia, New Zealand, the Commonwealth of Independent States, and East Asia.'[1] In a nutshell, across the developed world, freelancers report being happier in their work lives. This is

---

[1] https://s3.amazonaws.com/happiness-report/2017/HR17-Ch6_wAppendix.pdf

unsurprising. As a freelancer you have freedom and autonomy and are often better paid than you would be in full-time employment. And freelancing provides the most delightful sense of self-sufficiency.

What's less documented is how a freelance workforce can help close the gender gap and prevent the centralisation of societies. My evidence for this is more anecdotal.

One of main reasons women struggle to achieve board-level positions at the same rate as men is inequality (social, cultural, or judicial) in regard to childcare. Creating more freelance opportunities means that more families can have it all. Childcare is more easily shared if one or both parents can manage their own schedules. Both can stay at home and work, if they want. This goes some way to levelling the employment playing field. As freelance, remote working becomes commonplace, so will hiring freelance working parents. Likewise, as large corporations allow for flexible, remote working within their teams, and parents are actively encouraged to work with schedules that suit them, we can hope to see more balanced boards. With freelancing, opportunities for success are no longer exclusively tied to your physical ability to be in a certain place at a certain time, but on your ability to do your job. This could promote equality in the workplace in the long run.

I'm not a parent, but I'm proud to say that a large portion of my staff are, and they're able to look after their children and still work because of the opportunities flexible working has created for them.

When I tell people about my business model, people often ask me, 'But how do you manage a freelance team?', the assumption being that effective management is directly dependent on physical proximity. This simply isn't the case – trust me. I'd argue that for those who feel this way, their idea of management is too closely tied to the idea of productivity being represented by sitting at a desk staring seriously at a screen. If we stop considering simply showing up as a marker of positive professional output, and look only at the actual *work* someone is producing (whether it's a tangible deliverable or happy clients or more sales), then the management of a remote team becomes much more effective and aligned with overall objectives. Who cares if someone turned up at 9.30am rather than 9am if they're doing exactly what it is they're meant to be doing otherwise? If a job is being completed to the agreed standards in a reasonable timeframe, everything else is utterly arbitrary.

Of course, teams, and often more junior members of staff, can struggle to remain productive without the pressure of peer review, but only because we're so accustomed to having to be in a certain place at a certain time. The removal of this constraint fills us with a childlike joy, as if we're running onto the playground and smelling the fresh air for the first time. If we consciously remove the novelty of remote working and replace it with trust and training, the result is an adult-to-adult dynamic in our working relationships, which results in increased confidence, happiness, and productivity in our teams. If society stops treating employees like children, we'll stop acting like them (sometimes).

Likewise, as it becomes increasingly acceptable to work from home, there's less of a correlation between where we live and our earning potential. We no longer need to live in densely populated cities or the richest parts of the world to enjoy lucrative employment. If we continue to give people the flexibility to work from home and manage their own schedules, the miserable commute – rush hour traffic and unreliable public transport – can be a thing of the past. I fail to understand why in a modern, globally connected society we still think it appropriate to say, 'OK, office workers, can *all of you* try to get somewhere *at the same time*?' Whose wise idea was that? We're intentionally congesting our roads and public transport and making everyone absolutely bloody miserable. Whether you're employed or self-employed, we should all be striving to ensure workers have autonomy.

The reason that I managed to eventually to make my business profitable with zero capital or investment was because my team was, and still is, exclusively freelance. And freelancers are often the most talented people within an industry. Why? Because someone gets to a certain level in their career and realises they could make significantly more money doing for themselves what they're currently doing for someone else. As a result, many (not all) of the best people within an industry decide to go it alone. It can become an incredible slog for businesses to hold on to their good employees.

By extension, working with freelancers also means that you end up working with people who, for the most part, are entrepreneurial. They've taken risks and plunged into being freelance. This can often mean they rarely miss deadlines and the quality of their work is high. As we know, TF will ensure we continue delivering to a standard that keeps food on the table.

Another added bonus of working with freelancers is the total lack of internal politics. One of the most difficult things (I hear) about running a business with an employed team and an office space and a hierarchy and all of the things that go along with the traditional employment model is managing the internal politics and resulting drama. As freelancers work remotely, there's no hierarchy, and therefore no struggle to get promoted, or to be heard – absolutely zero politics. Instead, freelancers enjoy collaborating, as most of the time, they work alone. This breezy, drama-free, synergistic way of working is an absolute delight that I didn't see coming.

Once you find freelancers you can rely on, you'll be able to work with them for years, and you'll reap the benefits of having a world-class team with zero overhead and, thankfully, no office politics.

As a small business owner, working with a free-lance, remote team allowed me to grow and scale much more quickly than I could have otherwise. I was allowed to put the profit that would have otherwise been spent on office space towards expanding the team. I could take on new clients and be able to find the team to deliver the work quickly and smoothly without the huge risk, process and expense of formal hiring. If you're a small business looking to grow quickly, tapping in to the global pool of talented freelancers can be a great way to able to do this.

The point is not that freelancing and remote working will, or should, completely usurp traditional employment, as this offers structure and benefits that for many are a necessity, though we need to establish a culture of flexibility and autonomy where we allow the professional workforce, a collection of autonomous individuals with different styles and needs, the benefit of choosing how they can be the most happy and productive.

How to find the right freelancers

I've defined a few rules for myself over the years. They help me find the right people to work with and ensure that they want to work with me and can effectively collaborate with the rest of my team. These rules have been tried and tested through my own failures. If you want to work with freelancers, or if you're a freelancer wanting to get more work, I suggest considering the following.

Prioritise experience over cost

What makes a good freelancer is their ability to adapt quickly to different projects, manage their time, and be clear and direct. These skills are developed over time. I've consistently found that if you want a good freelancer, you want one with a lot of experience. An experienced freelancer will of course be more costly than a less experienced candidate, so be prepared to pay. It's considerably more expensive than hiring if they operate full time, but ultimately, there's less risk. A good freelancer is efficient and has years and years of experience behind them. Equally, if you prioritise keeping costs low, you're strongly increasing the chances of needing to pay to have the work done again.

Utilise recommendations

One of the most effective and reliable ways to find freelance resource is through others' recommendations. There are plenty of online freelance marketplaces, such as People Per Hour (www. peopleperhour.com) or Upwork (www.upwork. com), on which you can find freelancers across a huge range of disciplines at varying levels of cost and quality; of course, there's an unavoidable element of trial and error here. If you can get a recommendation from a colleague or peer you trust, essentially, you have somebody else removing a layer of trial and error for you. Personally, I've had success finding skilled freelancers through LinkedIn, either by searching skill sets I require directly or by sharing a status asking for recommendations from my network. But again, be prepared to spend a lot more time separating the wheat from the chaff, as it were, when using LinkedIn.

GO WITH 'CAREER' FREELANCERS RATHER THAN SPARE-TIME FREELANCERS

There are two distinct types of freelancers: those who do freelance work as a career (it's their day job) and those who do freelance work in their spare time (outside of their primary employment, to earn extra cash on the side).

I recommend working only with career freelancers. There are excellent spare-time freelancers, but whenever I've used them, the quality of the work is invariably lower, the turnaround times are slower, and deadlines are missed more often. This makes sense, of course. If your freelance revenue isn't essential to your living, and your time is already stretched between work and home commitments, any activities you commit to on the side won't be given priority, and this is more often than not reflected in the work produced. There will be exceptions to this, of course, but as a hard and fast rule, I say work only with those freelancers whose income and reputation is reliant on the revenue they generate for themselves.

Remember that if they miss deadlines the first time, they probably will again

This is something I've seen extensively over the past few years. Freelancers who miss their first deadline with me end up missing every deadline. There are extenuating circumstances occasionally, of course, so don't write off someone entirely for missing a deadline – but do proceed with caution. Wherever possible, I encourage the freelancers I work with to determine their own deadlines based on how long they think a project will take and their workload. This way, if the deadline is missed, it's a result of the freelancer's own time-management issue. If they're new to freelancing, they're likely in that familiar 'say yes to everything' phase, so you can more reliably try them again in good faith. If not, however, I'd be reluctant to invest a lot of time or resources in this person again, particularly if missed deadlines have a direct negative impact on your business.

Recognise the value of email invites

This is perhaps my most specific rule. You can tell a lot from this single action. If someone reaches out to me, wanting to work with me, and they send me a meeting invite after I schedule a meeting to discuss the project, I find this to be a surprisingly strong and reliable indicator of someone who's organised and committed to doing a good job. I acknowledge how arbitrary this may seem, but when you need to decipher reliability quickly, it's amazing what you notice.

Trust your freelancers

My business relies entirely on my freelancers' *wanting* to work with me. This means I need to treat them well – that is, I need to respect their independence, their expertise, and their decision to work for themselves. Having been on both sides of the spectrum, I know that too many people treat their freelancers like employees; they manage their schedules, double-check their time, and don't trust them to work alone. The freelancer–employer relationship isn't hierarchical. Your freelancers likely have plenty of work and opportunity, so don't treat them otherwise. Those working with freelancers don't have the power, especially if they're relying on the output of a freelancer to manage a project or deliver something they're almost certainly making a profit on. The best freelancer–employer relationships are mutual, adult-to-adult relationships where the freelancer is trusted to invoice fairly and complete the work as efficiently as possible. If you have a strong hunch that a freelancer isn't trustworthy, rather than wasting time and effort trying to micromanage them, just find others whom you can trust.

PAY ON TIME

This should go without saying, but sadly, it needs to be said. Always pay your freelancers in line with your initial terms. Pay early, if you can. Don't be that person who creates cash-flow problems for someone else. Be generous and reliable with your freelancers, and they will be generous with their time and reliable with their deadlines in return.

Building a Team and a Culture

So you have your brilliant team. Now how do you get them to work together? They're likely a group of strangers who have never met, who work from different office spaces across the world, and who have different skill sets, motivations, and responsibilities.

I thought this would be the hardest element of developing Manyminds. I feared that my role in the business would mostly consist of trying to get several unwilling participants to interact – kind of like organising a British dinner party.

Thankfully, this hasn't been the case. The general isolation of freelancing, alongside the fact that freelancers aren't living together in an office-style environment and scrabbling for promotions, brings about a genuine enthusiasm to collaborate. It's been the happiest accident of my life to date – bringing together really smart people who want to do great shit together. Who knew!

Optimise this enthusiasm by bringing teams together in fun, new, exciting environments as often as possible. Hiring a cool meeting space and taking your remote teams out for dinner and drinks is always worth the investment.

Where possible, especially if you'll be working with them consistently or on a longer-term project, provide your freelancers with benefits, such as access to your office space, if you have one, or support during sick days. Sick days. Sick days are awful when you're a freelancer because they don't exist. This didn't occur to me until about two months after I started Manyminds. I got awful flu but still had to work because there was no one else. The buck stopped with me. Try to establish a framework where someone else can step in and everything won't fall apart if a freelancer is sick. Freelancers also often miss the perks of recognition that an office environment provides, but systems such as Perkbox will allow you to give recognition inexpensively.

Go out of your way whenever possible to help and to thank people. Make it a conscious effort. Whoever said that you have to be ruthless in business was an asshat – an incorrect asshat. There will be times when you need your freelancers to be flexible and to go out of their way for you, so replicate that. Be kind, patient, honest, and humble. I guarantee the nicer you are in your day-to-day life, the more you'll get back. Karma or something like that.

CREATING EFFECTIVE COMMUNICATION

The success of a remote business relies almost entirely on effective communication. Establish a process for conferences and meetings. This is something my team and I are still ironing out. We've tried multiple ways to systemise our communication (Hangouts, Skype, appear.in), and I think we've finally found solace in Slack and GoToMeeting. Make it clear from the beginning what channels your teams should be talking through to remove as many barriers to face-to-face (or camera-to-camera) communication as possible.

Equally, make room for informal, inane chat. The Manyminds Slack is 20% talking to clients on an ad hoc basis, 20% discussing projects as a team, and 60% silly memes. It's this informal, silly conversation that builds the team dynamic. Create separate spaces for it so that it doesn't distract from work, but make sure you have these spaces. I know a lot of business owners who get stressed out about their team 'wasting time' on instant messaging. This may be a more legitimate concern when everyone works together, but for remote teams, having the ability to do this is crucial. And it may well prevent a serious bout of potentially fatal solo afternoon karaoke.

Also, be sure to schedule regular check-in meetings – an allotted time when all the teams talk keeps things systemised and moving.

Developing processes

For me, developing processes has involved a steep learning curve. When you're servicing multiple clients, it's hard to take time out to develop something that doesn't seem immediately necessary. Here are some things I've started doing to take the sting out of something I'm not naturally adept at. (In fact, I hired someone to do some of these things for me, so, you know, there's always that too.)

Brief encounters (sorry)

Even the best freelancers in the world will deliver bad work if the brief is bad. My project manager once described me as 'horrible' at briefing. Harsh, but, OK, I can accept criticism. When I try to take what's in my head and distil it into a clear, detailed, informative document, the first few sentences are good and then the writing devolves into me repeatedly typing something along the lines of this: 'Do the thing, the thing I want, do it, do the thingy thing thing, please.

Two things by this day. Thank you for the things I envisage. GOODBYE!' But I've discovered a cheat (a hack, if you will): video briefing. Now I use Zoom to record myself discussing a project. I can provide a lot more details, it can be re-watched (unlike a phone call), and I can send it to my project manager to distil if necessary. Recording a quick briefing video takes significantly less time than typing one out.

PROCESS MAPS

I've recently started building process maps and have found them hugely helpful when working with a team of freelancers. Having multiple scenarios for what someone does in a given situation has reduced my time spent answering questions. One of the specific problems in my team was client contact ownership. I generally manage a lot of the client relationships, but I can't always be readily available or know the right answers, so there was a little confusion and hesitation around who was accountable. A distinct process map solved this quickly.

SHARED FOLDERS

In all the mayhem of the business set-up, my team and I didn't get all of our documentation organised so that it was available to everyone. Now, we use shared folders in Google Drive. When people are working remotely, it's essential to have everything organised and readily available, particularly for anyone new to the team. A lot of documentation ends up being saved on freelancers' desktops – there needs to be a process to prevent this.

SHADOW STAFF

A crucial expense. You need to ensure that if a remote team is no longer able to work on a project, there's not a huge gap in resources. Even if a project requires only one freelancer, you need to be paying for two, just in case. Again, don't scrimp.

TASK MANAGEMENT

Everything needs to be documented, itemised, and assigned to different people across the teams with full visibility. This is important. We use Asana, which integrates with Instagantt beautifully for reports. Well, I say 'We use Asana', but I'm the worst on the team for being consistent with it, which really annoys my project manager. Oh, and don't annoy your project manager.

CHAPTER EIGHT
A WORLD OF OPPORTUNITY

A lot of this book has focused on the more negative, or realistic, aspects of freelancing. But as I said earlier, going freelance has had such huge positive impact on other areas of my life.

WHY FREELANCING CAN MAKE YOU HAPPIER

One of the most unquestionably delightful elements of being your own boss is getting to work to your own rhythm, according to your mood and energy level. I'm one of those elusive morning people. From 7am until about 11am I'm focused, enthused, and effective. At about 11am I start to get bored and will usually eat an early lunch, then fall into some YouTube hole about how to get the perfect eyebrow arch. I can then pull myself back to work for a couple of hours, until I regress to lazy-toddler mode at about 4pm.

This is when I'll take a short nap or get started on dinner. I'll typically do some lighter work in the evenings, if I'm in the mood. The great thing is that I can work my patterns to my productive advantage, rather than trying to fight them. I don't have to stare at a screen in a brightly lit office, eyes burning. Getting into a non-nine-to-five rhythm takes time, as you have to unlearn everything you learned about working times and routines and structure from the day you started school. But shaking off the guilt of not following the exact path you were prescribed as a child can be the most rewarding element of managing your own time.

In the two years of working for myself, I've travelled to more countries and more places than I have in my entire life. I've been able to work where I want, when I want, and while this often comes with crippling fear, it has opened up a world of opportunity and freedom.

Here's a nice example. About a year after starting my business, I was completely consumed by TF. I'd officially shed my human skin and replaced it with sweatpants and a hoodie. My life had become work; I would never switch off and was visibly burning out. I was working from home alone, so, like some sad business Macaulay Culkin, I'd often go days without leaving the house or speaking to another human face-to-face. I'd just sit in my kitchen and work, not looking up from my computer until it was dark outside. My only human interactions were crackly, disjointed Skype calls with my clients.

Then, a year later, I got invited to speak at a conference in San Diego. Fate, or coincidence, whichever you prefer, would have it that one of my closest friends happened to be working in San Francisco at the time. Based on her justified concern about my new work-only lifestyle, she urged me to take some time off, and we arranged a trip across California. I was almost excited, though genuine excitement was hindered by grave concern about accessing reliable Wi-Fi.

The first night, we went to watch some music in a bar called the Boom Boom Room. The band was awful. I got very drunk and stood at the front of the crowd feeling disgruntled that I wasn't in London, where the good bands and reliable Wi-Fi were.

A handsome American with a beard and turquoise-rimmed circular spectacles, a hipster-Victorian-academic type, came to talk to us. I wasn't interested and continued being drunk and disgruntled, like the good Brit I am. Then he mentioned that he'd quit his reliable job in the wine industry to focus on his passions: music and motorbikes. I remember being surprised and admiring his gumption and spirit to go it alone, especially in a society where financial and employment success is closely tied to self-worth. We went outside to smoke and spoke at length about Cream and San Francisco's homeless problem. At about 4am, after the bar had closed, Claudia and I left. When the American messaged me asking me to come to his hotel to keep chatting, I remember sleepily putting my phone on silent, thinking, *They're all the same.*

I woke up to several messages from him, the verbalised confidence crisis of a drunk man turned sober.

'I'd like to see you before you leave California.'

Weird, I thought.

'OK,' I said.

Three days later, he invited me to the shed where he was building his motorbike. And so I found myself in an Uber on my way into the mountains of Sonoma Valley. My friend was (legitimately) concerned and frustrated.

The drive into the mountains was absurd and beautiful. I'd been drinking wine all day and the sun was shining, and I didn't have a clue what was going on or what I was doing or whom I was meeting. It was the middle of the day, and for the first time since going freelance, I was *relishing* the freedom that being your own boss can bring.

The Uber driver, a friendly woman called Margo, had never driven along the winding road up into the mountains before, and I could see she was getting a little apprehensive as the road thinned and weaved through the trees along steep edges that led to the valley hundreds of feet (probably) below. I felt a little guilty, but at this stage there was nothing I could do. Not only did I not have reliable Wi-Fi, this place was so remote I didn't even have signal. I distinctly remember how dangerously thrilling this felt – to be completely uncontactable felt perilous! Then I caught myself and thought about how pitiful I'd become.

I arrived and said a stifled hello to the Victorian Academic, and he introduced me to his friend, Peter. I recall that the introduction of a third party surprised me and also made me feel mildly despondent. I wasn't exactly there to find a pen pal. Five rather strained minutes later, however, I learned Peter was a developer who ran his own business, so we enjoyed a breezy conversation about work. I gladly found myself in familiar territory, talking about server configuration, in an unfamiliar setting (a small shed in the woods).

An hour later, my tipsy excitement was replaced by awkward boredom, and I began laying down the appropriate courtesies to pave my departure. I took out my phone to order an Uber back into town and then remembered I was in the woods in the mountains with absolutely zero signal. I would have had more success hooting the mating call of a mountain lion and returning to civilisation on its back.

Shortly after, a car pulled up. A woman got out and walked towards the small shed containing three drunk strangers, a half-built motorbike, and palpable tension.

As she continued to walk towards us, I become increasingly awkward. Already feeling incredibly out of place, I couldn't bring myself to leave the confines of the little shed to introduce myself. Being British, I need at least six weeks' warning that I'll have to engage in social courtesies.

I conducted a swift mental scan of my options and did the only thing a successful, cogent, confident, well-rounded adult can do in a socially awkward situation.

I pretended to read.

I pretended to read a handbook for motorcycle mechanics.

I pretended to read it as if I were a fourteenth-century monk poring over a sacred manuscript. I pretended to read more intently than I've ever read in my life. I'm not even sure I blinked. If I could have harvested that desperation to stare at a page without breaking focus during my university education, I probably never would have found myself in a shed in the mountains.

As I desperately pretended to read, I overheard something about dinner. Oh no, not dinner. Anything but dinner. Take me round the back and chop me to bits, but please don't make me have dinner.

I'm going to have to look up, I thought. *It's gone too far. I'm being offered dinner by the man I met in bar who I came to drink wine with but his friend was here so I've been drinking with his friend because Victorian Academic hasn't spoken a word and I'm staring at this manual like a teenage boy staring at his first nipple.*

Moments before I folded my business to fully redefine myself as a motorcycle mechanic, I realised I needed to step in. I looked up, my neck stiff with reluctance and my soul screaming to leave, and gushingly, warmly, and enthusiastically accepted dinner.

We went inside the main house, a beautiful cottage surrounded by trees. I felt so awkward. *I have no idea what I'm doing here, I have no way to get home, and I'm suddenly very drunk.*

I drank wine.

We drank so much wine, and ate pasta and cheese, and the conversation began to flow and I started to have a really nice time. As we all spoke about collective consciousness and listened to the Beatles, Victorian Academic held my hand under the table.

Later, I got on the ropey Wi-Fi and ordered that Uber. As the car headed down the winding hills, I smiled as I thought about what had been perhaps one of the most spontaneous and delightful evenings of my life.

Three weeks after arriving home, and to the great amusement of my flatmate, I booked a flight back to San Francisco, and flew out two days later. I did this in part because I wanted to see him again, but mainly just because I *could*. I'd worked my ass off for two years and I was finally allowing myself to exercise, and revel in, the total personal freedom that being freelance affords, and the ability I'd created for myself to travel across the world on a whim.

As I boarded the flight to San Francisco on the off-chance a guy I met once might want to go for a drink, I distinctly recall putting my bag in the hold and giggling to myself. This was just one big silly adventure and I was having the time of my life.

I landed in San Francisco, jumped in an Uber, and picked a hotel at random.

I woke up the next morning still unsure whether I was actually going to see him. I decided to call a client to manage the guilt of my desertion, and when I got off the phone, I saw that he'd messaged me, asking when we could meet up. It was only about 7.30am, and his eagerness made me smile.

We were married three months later.

We spent the summer in California and then decided to move back to the UK. California is eight hours behind, and at the time, 90% of my clients were UK-based. I didn't want to wake up every day feeling behind and needing to get through a swathe of emails. I can say with absolute certainty that I never, ever, would have met and married Connor without being freelance. Being your own boss creates freedom and self-sufficiency that opens so many new doors.

Despite TF and the difficulty of switching off, going freelance has been, by far, the most positive thing I've ever done for myself, and my quality of life. I can travel the world and work in different continents, stay out late if my night is going well (without worrying about the repercussions of a dastardly commute), and move home for short stints when my family need me to.

Be prepared for and aware of the stress that it can bring, but if you have the chance and feel so inclined, I implore you to work for yourself, and to allow those in your employment to have the same experience.

I hope that you've found this book helpful or inspiring in some way. And I hope that at the very least, reading about my mistakes has given you some reassurance that deciding to take the first step is a success in and of itself, that making mistakes does not mean you're a failure and that you don't need to be *at* work to *do* work.

I hope that this book has encouraged you to embrace flexible working in some way, and to award yourself a little more freedom, a little more patience, and a lot more kindness. And I hope that it has taught you, as the famous saying goes, that if at first you don't succeed, just wing it.

Thank you for taking the time to read this and I am excited to see you in our future freelance utopia – bring Wi-Fi.

ACKNOWLEDGEMENTS

As a collection of experiences and anecdotes, this book simply would not exist without the people who have shared these experiences with me and I would like to thank them for supporting me with their time, advice and patience.

Thanks must go to my business partner Tom, for keeping me sane and solvent; to my friend and ex-business wife Lexi, for being gracious and understanding. My best friends Jamie and Claudia: Jamie, warm thanks for always telling me when I am awful; Claudia, thank you for being the ultimate reason I have a job.

Thanks to Ian, for being a true friend, always believing in me, and being the *actual* reason my business exists; to Lynne, simply for the innuendos. Thanks to my perpetual cheerleader and life-long pen pal Alice, and to my suffering flat mate Jen, for making me book the flight. Thank you, Jono, for being the first eyes on the first chapter and the first person to tell me it might be interesting. Joe, thank you for being the world's best client, for the weekly calls and lunch-time sushi – you made running a business really bloody fun. Thank you, Kieran, for being my oldest, closest friend and answering the phone when I sobbed in stairwells in the early days.

Thank you to every single freelancer I have had the pleasure of working with, though especially Pam, Dan, Oli, Tom, and of course Josh, who coolly dealt with the absolute worst version of me on a daily basis. Thank you to all of my clients for putting food on the table and being a delight to work with (for, you know, the most part). Thank you to my family for teaching me, through their very real examples of absurd behaviour, to not care what people think; and to Connor, whose support, encouragement and impatience got me, kicking and screaming, to the finish line.

The Author

Kirsty is the founder and managing director of Manyminds, a digital marketing agency that works exclusively with freelancers in remote teams across the world. With clients ranging from global blue chips to small startups, Kirsty has truly disrupted the way companies outsource their marketing efforts.

With over a decade's experience defining digital strategies for some of the world's biggest brands, she is a recognised digital expert and has spoken at conferences across the world on digital innovation and leadership.

She has recently turned her limited attention span to promoting the benefits of freelance teams and remote working, both for employers and the self-employed. Helping businesses develop the processes and structures required to allow their teams to work remotely, she hopes to encourage more companies to reap the rewards of a flexible, freelance workforce.

She lives in Birmingham with her husband and their baby daughter, Amazon Alexa.

SOCIAL MEDIA

www.kirstyhulse.com
Twitter: @kirsty_hulse
Kirsty@manyminds.digital